THE LIMITS OF THE MARKET

PAUL DE GRAUWE

THE LIMITS OF
THE MARKET

The Pendulum between Government
and Market

TRANSLATED BY
ANNA ASBURY

OXFORD
UNIVERSITY PRESS

OXFORD
UNIVERSITY PRESS

Great Clarendon Street, Oxford, OX2 6DP,
United Kingdom

Oxford University Press is a department of the University of Oxford.
It furthers the University's objective of excellence in research, scholarship,
and education by publishing worldwide. Oxford is a registered trade mark of
Oxford University Press in the UK and in certain other countries

Published in the United States of America by Oxford University Press
198 Madison Avenue, New York, NY 10016, United States of America

British Library Cataloguing in Publication Data
Data available

Library of Congress Control Number: 2016945123

ISBN 978-0-19-878428-9

Printed in Great Britain by
CPI Group (UK) Ltd, Croydon, CRO 4YY

Flemish
Literature
Fund

This book was published with the support of the Flemish
Literature Fund (www.flemishliterature.be).

CONTENTS

LIST OF FIGURES

LIST OF TABLES

LIST OF BOXES

PREFACE

Until the 1980s intense debates raged in universities as to whether the economy needed managing by market mechanisms or government planning, a question of market vs state, each side with its own convinced supporters. It had to be one or the other.

We have since learnt a number of lessons. Firstly, a centrally planned economy does not work. Nowhere has such an economy succeeded in creating sufficient material prosperity for the population. This is the reason almost all communist regimes collapsed in the 1980s.

The second insight is that pure market systems do not exist anywhere. All known economic systems are a mixture of market and government control, and with good reason. A pure market system does not guarantee material prosperity for large segments of the population, which become marginalized and are left to their fate.

Pure market systems and purely centrally planned systems are therefore nowhere to be seen in the real world for the same fundamental reason. Neither succeeds in creating material prosperity for a large proportion of the population (in the case of a market economy) or even for the population as a whole (in the case of a centrally planned economy). Nor will people accept either system, unless they are maintained by a dictatorship, as in North Korea, for example. The age-old discussion of market vs state is therefore outdated. It cannot be one or the other. A mixture will always be required.

The only relevant question, then, is how precisely that mixture should look. How far should we let the market go in order to create as much prosperity as possible? What is the responsibility of the government in generating wealth? Who should do what to advance prosperity for all? These are awkward questions, but they are the only interesting ones, which is why we seek to tackle them in this book.

By formulating the problem in this way, we can circumvent many of the ideological positions on the subject. Markets are not inherently better or worse than governments. The only thing that counts is people's prosperity. Market and government are instruments for achieving that goal. There is therefore no point in being an advocate of the market in an absolute sense, any more than it makes sense to trust governments more than markets. Both are needed to promote prosperity.

That coveted mixture of market and state, however, is anything but easy to achieve. It is an arduous, sometimes destructive process, which is constantly in motion. There have been periods in history in which the market has gained increasing importance, recent decades being a good example. In other periods things moved in the opposite direction and governments gained in dominance. The turning points in these pendulum swings have coincided with disruptive events which test the boundaries of market and state. It is as if humanity in its search for the correct balance continually swings from one extreme to the other. The reason behind this dynamic is an important theme of this book.

We will also investigate the question of the dangers of these great historic shifts. Will the current movement, with the market gaining a greater role due to globalization, not bring it up against its limits? Or do the financial crisis and growing inequality of income and wealth show that we are already reaching those limits? What will happen then? Should we brace ourselves for the overthrow of the capitalist system? Will we return to an economy in which the government is in charge? Will this promote prosperity? These are among the many important questions I hope to answer in this book. They are also very topical questions, as witnessed for instance by the fierce discussions on increasing inequality of income and whether or not to introduce a tax on wealth.

This book also reflects my search for the truth. There have been moments in my life when I firmly believed that the market could offer a solution to most economic problems and that governments should play a minimal role. I have since withdrawn from that position. I believe I am now less ideologically driven and tend to think more pragmatically about the role which market and government should fulfil. Pragmatism also better enables us to think objectively about the ever-changing role which market and government play in society.

Without Lieven Sercu and Maarten Van Steenbergen, director and publisher at Lannoo, this book would never have come into being. They began to torment me several years ago with requests for a book on the subject. I did not feel inclined to write one, so I kept them waiting, but they persisted until I gave in and started working. The more I wrote the more enthusiastic I became. It was a thoroughly enriching personal experience, because it compelled me to order my ideas and look for new ones. Kris van Hamme, editor at Lannoo, read the first versions of this book with great patience. His critical mind has helped me to rectify errors and inaccuracies to make this book more readable.

This book is a translation from the Dutch (*De Limieten van de Markt*). A new chapter was added (Chapter 10) in which I discuss what economists and philosophers wrote about the relationship between market and state. I am very grateful to Anna Asbury for an excellent translation and to Howard Emmens for editing this book.

As well as footnotes (denoted by a symbol) the book includes numbered endnotes which are to be found at the end of the book.

CHAPTER 1

THE GREAT ECONOMIC PENDULUM

The economic history of the last two hundred years is one of cyclical movements, movements which increased the influence of the markets at the expense of governments, then returned the upper hand to governments at the expense of the markets.

The nineteenth century saw a protracted expansion of the capitalist system. Imitating Great Britain, which fired the starting shot for the process of liberalization in the eighteenth century, more and more countries on the continent of Europe dismantled internal restrictions inhibiting the free initiative of entrepreneurs. These entrepreneurs took advantage of the move to develop a multitude of new activities. External impediments to the free movement of goods and services were also cut back, enabling countries to specialize. International trade flourished.

The triumph of the market system was visible everywhere. Production of goods and services increased spectacularly in the countries which had deregulated their economic system. Material prosperity, as measured by per capita gross domestic product (per capita GDP), began to increase in Western Europe and America. That growth was made possible by entrepreneurs and capitalists tirelessly searching for new products and production methods. Competition between entrepreneurs led to an extraordinary dynamic of technological progress. The railways, electricity, telegraphy, and many other technological innovations drove material progress. This meant a doubling in prosperity in these two parts of the world by the end of the nineteenth century compared with 1800. For the first time in history the shackles

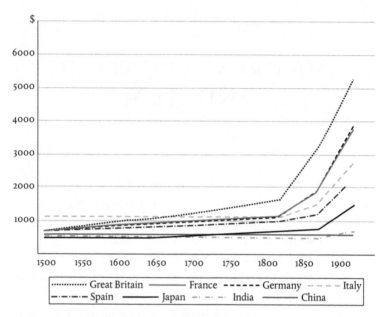

Figure 1.1. Per capita GDP in dollars (constant prices)

Source: Angus Maddison, *Contours of the World Economy, 1–2030 AD: Essays in Macro-Economic History* (Oxford: Oxford University Press, 2007), p. 382, Table A.7

of economic stagnation were thrown off (see Figure 1.1). There appeared to be no limits to the domain of the markets.

The First Half of the Twentieth Century: Decline of the Market

Those limits, however, were to become clear in the twentieth century. After the temporary interruption to growth in prosperity during World War I (along with the inexpressible suffering of millions), in the 1920s the unbridled expansion of capitalism appeared set to continue. However, that was not the case. In the 1930s the Great Depression set in. In many countries prosperity dropped dramatically, while unemployment rose to unprecedented levels. Millions of people in the most prosperous countries of Western Europe and America had suddenly lost their way and were plunged into the depths of misery. This immediately created a breeding ground for political extremism and violence, causing the collapse of democratic systems. It would eventually lead to the most horrifying war in history.

The triumphal procession of the market system came to an abrupt halt. In many countries people blamed the economic misery on the unbridled expansion of capitalism. Countries such as the Soviet Union had already turned their backs on the market system at the start of the 1920s and founded economies centrally led by government. They became the new trendsetters. In many countries the domain of the markets shrank and governments resolutely took over economic leadership. In the United States President Franklin Roosevelt launched his 'New Deal', a government programme aimed at rescuing the economy through large-scale government investments. In Germany the Nazi government did the same when it came to power in 1933, with great success in fact. In many countries the government became the institution which took over the decisions about investments from the markets. Key industries were nationalized. Countries closed their economic borders. It appeared that the market system was on the retreat and the future belonged to countries with government-controlled economies.

After World War II growth recovered, mainly due to government-driven rebuilding of Western economies. Government investment was the motor of growth. Public investments and construction of social security systems gave Western European governments a central place in the new economic model. The perception that the market system had failed to guarantee a decent existence for all drove governments to develop social security systems to protect the millions who were unemployed, sick, or disabled.

The growing significance of governments was also apparent from the increase in government spending in the post-war period. In Figure 1.2 we see the development of post-war government spending (up to 1990) in the countries that are members of the Organization for Economic Co-operation and Development (OECD). These are the

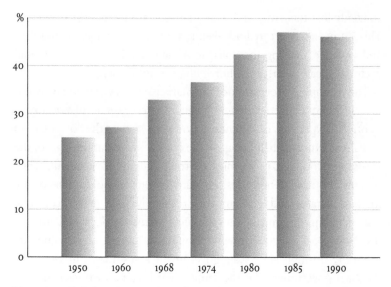

Figure 1.2. Global government spending in OECD countries (in % GDP)

most industrialized countries, largely in Europe and America. As shown, in the period between 1950 and 1985 government spending as a proportion of GDP in OECD countries almost doubled. This trend stopped after the mid-1980s.

Taxes on the highest incomes also rose substantially, as shown in Figure 1.3. In countries such as the UK and US the income of top earners was almost completely siphoned off, with tax rates of ninety per cent or more on the highest incomes, reflecting a widespread view that the rich do not really contribute to economic prosperity. This flew in the face of the fundamentals of market thinking, namely that successful people contribute a great deal to material prosperity. According to this view (the 'trickle-down theory') the poor in a country benefit from the initiatives of the few who amass large fortunes. The rich should be pampered and protected, to everyone's benefit. This theory was thrown out after the Great Depression.

For many people in the post-war period the rise of governments as the controllers of economies seemed an inevitable and permanent

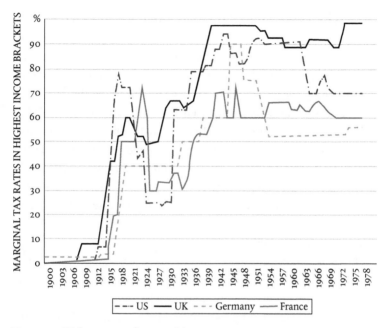

Figure 1.3. Highest rates of personal income tax
Source: Piketty, <http://piketty.pse.ens.fr/en/capital21c2>

fact. Many people saw the superiority of centrally planned economies as self-evident. In the famous 1959 Kitchen Debate between Richard Nixon, then vice president of the United States, and Nikita Khrushchev, then leader of the Soviet Union, Khrushchev declared with great conviction that the Soviet Union would catch up with the US before the end of the century. Many people were indeed convinced that this would happen. The famous American economist Paul Samuelson who received the Nobel Prize in 1970 was also the author of the most popular and influential economics textbook. The 1967 edition included an extrapolation of GDP per capita in the US and in the Soviet Union showing that by 1995 the Soviet Union would have caught up and surpassed the US. In later editions this catch-up moment was pushed further into the future, until the 1985 edition dropped this extrapolation altogether. Six years later the Soviet Union collapsed.

The 1980s: The Return of the Market System

Once again, history was to take a different turn. From the 1970s it became increasingly clear that government-controlled economies were reaching their limits. Countries which had gone the furthest in government control were experiencing the greatest difficulties in achieving economic progress. They suffered from a lack of technological innovation. Nationalized companies and sectors suffered great losses, which had to be made up through taxes. Economies in the Soviet Union and Eastern Europe stagnated and there were serious shortages of essential goods and services. For all those with their eyes open, it was clear that government-managed economies failed to create material prosperity.

The cause of this failure is now clear to everyone (although this was not the case in the post-war period). The central planner issues instructions to countless companies stating what and how much they should manufacture, whom to buy materials from, what machines to use, how many workers to employ, what salaries to pay and prices to charge, where the products should be transported to, what the retail prices should be, and thousands of other details. An organizational model of this kind runs into two problems.

The first relates to information. In order to issue all these instructions, information on all manufacturing options and methods must be centrally available, along with the preferences of millions of consumers. That is an enormous mountain of data that also changes constantly. In reality it proved impossible to keep all that information up to date, process it, and make use of it. The consequence was that the wrong goods and services were produced and ended up in the wrong places, leading to large surpluses in some places and shortages elsewhere. The long queues in front of the shops in Moscow became the symbol of the great inefficiency of a centrally planned economy.

A second problem is that the centrally planned economic model provides too little incentive for effort and creativity. People who receive instructions must follow them to the letter, at the risk of being punished. They do only what is asked of them and nothing more. The subsequent lack of experimentation with new products or manufacturing methods results in technological stagnation. Products and technologies remained unchanged for half a century in Eastern Europe and the Soviet Union. A particularly spectacular example was exposed when East Germany opened up, as the Zeiss camera factories in Jena had not changed any aspect of their products since World War II. They were still using the same old technology, while the Japanese had been constantly introducing new cameras with advanced new technical features into the market at breakneck speed.

The failure of government management of the economy led to a liberalization movement from America and the United Kingdom taking much of the world in its grip. Markets all over the world opened up once again. Governments owning a large part of the economy privatized public companies. Telecom companies, railways, car manufacturers, banks, and water companies which had been nationalized over the last few decades were privatized again.

Countries reopened their borders. World trade was liberalized, setting the stage for enormous globalization of the economy. Countries such as China and the Soviet Union threw their principles of central management overboard and converted to capitalism. They may have maintained state-owned enterprises, but their share of national production dropped steadily. Private companies were now the source of economic dynamism.

Just as in the nineteenth century, this was seen as a triumph for the market system. Material prosperity in the countries which had liberated their economies underwent incredible growth. This was most spectacular in the countries of East Asia, which began to grow by ten per cent per year from the 1960s (Japan), 1970s (Korea), and 1980s (China). This spectacular growth enabled countries such as Japan and Korea to approach the prosperity levels of America and Western Europe. China still has a long way to go, but it is already clear that the country has succeeded in raising the prosperity of the population to unprecedented levels (by Chinese standards) at record speed.

The Market Reaches Everything

The rise of the market system since the 1980s has not only led to spectacular growth in material prosperity in countries which until recently lived in the greatest poverty. That rise also manifested itself in another way: market mechanisms and principles increasingly crept into areas of society where they were previously absent.

There are myriad examples of this effect. In more and more countries education, especially higher education, became subject to market principles. Fees for universities in many countries rose steeply. The professors, who previously enjoyed academic freedom (in many cases meaning doing what they liked to do without any checks from society), became subject to the same evaluation criteria as employees in the private sector. Academics who performed well and published a great deal came to receive higher rewards than those who failed to do so.

The cultural sector did not escape this trend either. Where in the past theatres were able to count on government support for a large proportion of their finances, many had to look elsewhere. Increasingly directors went in search of financial support from sponsors and theatregoers instead of the taxpayer.

Within companies, too, a revolution took place. Businesses were in fact organizations governed by hierarchical structures. The boss gave orders and the employees followed their instructions. This often led to a lack of involvement and creativity among employees. Now companies were increasingly driven to follow market principles even internally. Bonuses were required to incentivize efforts on the part of employees in the hope that these would lead to better performance. Another way of introducing market principles was outsourcing. Activities which the company itself would traditionally carry out were contracted out to external businesses, playing them off against one another to supply services more cheaply than the company itself could do.

The market triumphed everywhere and broadened its radius of action. Capitalism once again seemed unstoppable, with nothing to prevent its rise. Then came the crisis of 2008.

8

This short historical overview shows that there are limits to the expansion of the market system. Sometimes the dynamics of the system seem unstoppable, particularly because it generates material wealth as no other system can, but it repeatedly stumbles on limits and falls victim to its own success. At that moment governments step in, and political management and control become important again. Over time, however, government management systems also reach their limits. It is as if market and government are locked in a perpetual battle, attempting to win ground from one another, overthrowing the other again and again.

What limitations keep on halting the rise of the markets? What makes governments repeatedly withdraw from the economy? Are we condemned to repeat this cyclical movement of market and government expansion ad infinitum, or is it possible to achieve a magical balance between the two? These are the questions we will explore in this book.

CHAPTER 2

THE LIMITS OF CAPITALISM

The success of capitalism in advancing material prosperity is overwhelming. The many attempts to organize the economy in ways other than the market mechanism have failed. The enormous difference between capitalist and communist approaches to the economy is clear from the contrast between North and South Korea, which provide us with a natural experiment for evaluating the effect of two economic organizations.

After the Korean War in the 1950s the country was split in two. North Korea organized its economy according to the Soviet model of central planning. South Korea adopted the principles of the market economy. The effect of this split on the material prosperity of the two countries was spectacular (see Figure 2.1). In 1950 both countries were equally poor. From the 1970s, however, per capita GDP in South Korea exploded, while in North Korea it stagnated. The consequence was that in 2007 per capita GDP in South Korea was nearly twenty times that in North Korea.

There are countless examples of the spectacular success of capitalism in generating material progress, the most obvious probably being China. When the country resolutely opted for the path of capitalism after Mao's death, the Chinese economy began to grow at a pace of ten per cent or more per year. Today China is the second largest economy in the world and hundreds of millions of Chinese people have been raised from the depths of starvation, which claimed the lives of millions of people every year in previous millennia.

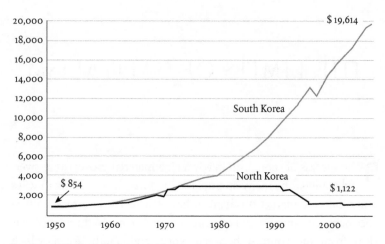

Figure 2.1. Real GDP per capita in North and South Korea

Source: Angus Maddison, *Contours of the World Economy, 1–2030 AD: Essays in Macro-Economic History* (Oxford: Oxford University Press, 2007), p. 382, Table A.7

Praise for Capitalism

Where does this capitalist success come from? That is the first question we should address, as the answer will enable us to study the central question of this chapter, why capitalism appears to have limits.

The success of capitalism is all about its decentralized character. Consumers decide autonomously how much and what to consume. Companies decide how much and what to produce. No one tells them what to do. Nevertheless these decisions are coordinated in markets where demand is confronted with supply of goods and services. If there is more demand than supply, prices rise. This has a double effect: higher prices lead consumers to buy less while encouraging companies to produce more. They do this not out of love for the consumer but out of a desire to increase their own profit. This self-regulatory mechanism eventually leads to the fulfilment of consumer demand.

This decentralized system, moreover, creates a dynamic whereby entrepreneurs are constantly searching for new products and services, as well as cheaper production methods, again not out of love for the consumer, but in order to maximize their own profit. When new products and services catch on, entrepreneurs can make higher profits. Cheaper production methods enable them to cut costs, lower prices, and attract more consumers, again raising profits. This mechanism explains why capitalism is a system in which there is constant technological progress, forming the basis for spectacular advances in material prosperity.

The dynamics of the market system led the great eighteenth-century Scottish economist Adam Smith to the conclusion that there was effectively an 'invisible hand' ensuring that firms' efforts to promote their own interests automatically lead to the promotion of general well-being. The baker who gets up at four in the morning to bake bread is not acting out of altruism; it is to increase profits. This individual calculation ensures that we have fresh bread each morning, in other words that the consumer's well-being is served.

This insight from Adam Smith was revolutionary, effectively stating that the collective interest is best served when everyone strives to satisfy their own interests, thus reconciling individual rationality with collective rationality. What is good for the individual is good for the entire group. If that is the case, no one can really be against such a system. So why is there so much resentment, even resistance, to this system? This leads us to the question of the limits of capitalism.

Individual and Collective Rationality

The limits of a market system relate to the fact that the connection between individual and collective rationality can be severed. That connection is broken when millions of people searching for their own interest does not lead to a situation perceived to be optimal by everyone. How do such situations arise?

In this book we will explore a number of these situations. I group them into two categories. The first I call *external limits*. These relate to the fact that an individual's decisions often have a positive or negative influence on others which the individual does not take into consideration. Economists call these externalities or external effects. These are individual decisions which are not really individual because they directly affect the prosperity of others. A market system does not take these externalities into account because the actors in this system (consumers and companies) are not rewarded for doing so.

Let us clarify this with an example, to which we will return in detail in later chapters. If a company produces steel, it also produces harmful chemicals which it releases into the air or water. This is a cost borne by people outside the steel company. For instance, nearby residents may inhale harmful chemicals, so that their health suffers and they die prematurely. Those who do not die immediately become ill and less productive, and so on. None of these costs are taken into account when the company calculates the cost of a tonne of steel, so the price of the steel will not reflect these external costs. In fact the steel is cheaper than it should be, resulting in excessive demand. This leads to the important conclusion that what is good for the individual steel manufacturer and for individual buyers of cheap steel is bad for many other people. Individual rationality does not coincide with collective rationality.

We will investigate a number of other examples of such external effects which lead to a discrepancy between individual and collective rationality. When they diverge sufficiently this causes resistance to a system which is not succeeding in guaranteeing prosperity for all. Individual success is then insufficient to maintain support from society for the market system.

Systems I and II

There is a second category of situations which lead to a rift between individual and collective rationality. These are the *internal limits* of the free market system.

The free market system appeals to individual rationality, the calculation aimed at determining an individual person's best interest. The market system is therefore based on an image of humanity which economists term 'homo economicus', applied to individuals who are constantly calculating what best serves their own interests.

Psychologists, however, have discovered that every individual possesses another dimension at odds with the calculating aspect of their character. A well-known representative of this stance is Daniel Kahneman, an Israeli psychologist who won the Nobel Prize for Economics in 2002 for his groundbreaking work on the influence of irrational behaviour on the economy. He developed the idea that there are two systems at work in our brains.[1] System I relates to intuitive, emotional behaviour and is the oldest in evolutionary terms, governing emotions of fear, panic, euphoria, sympathy, disgust, and so on. It is also the system which regulates emotions such as love and the desire for fairness.

System II is the rational, calculating part of the human mind. It is the system which causes us to weigh up what is best for our well-being, making a cost-benefit analysis before we come to a decision. In contrast with System I, which can lead to very quick decisions (fear of danger causes us to run away immediately, for example), System II is slow. Under System II we line up many different factors which might affect our well-being before coming to a decision. That requires time and effort. Often we are unwilling to make that effort. According to Kahneman, System II is 'lazy', which can lead to individuals potentially making insufficiently rational calculations and being led by System I (the emotional system) in decision-making processes.

The two systems are connected, requiring balance. Antonio Damasio[2] has shown that if individuals work with the rational system (System II) alone, without generating any emotion (System I), they also make very poor decisions which work against their own interest. The two systems constantly interact. If one gains the upper hand at the expense of the other, things go wrong.

We now come to the core of the internal limits of the market system. This mainly calls on the rational System II inside us. There is nothing wrong with that per se, but the fact that the market almost exclusively uses System II leads to an internal conflict in individuals. An individual encouraged to activate just one system, while setting the other aside, feels unhappy and unable to develop properly as a human being. Being asked to develop their skills as homo economicus, and rewarded by the market with a good income, does not make people happy. Their many other desires, such as love and fairness, are not satisfied by the way they are rewarded by the market. In fact the market system is completely indifferent to these desires (although see Box 2.1, in which we point out that clever marketers have discovered the importance of System I, using it to sell their products).

A distributional problem also arises. In a pure market system only individual performance is rewarded. People who cannot perform because they are sick or disabled receive nothing and are essentially left to die. The market system is indifferent to this outcome. Whether the distribution of income is fair or not is of no importance to the market system. For many people who are well rewarded by the market, this leads to an internal conflict between System I, which also recognizes a sense of fairness, and System II, which is content with the outcome of the system.

In some sense the limits of the market system are more fundamental here. We call these limits *internal* because the pressure of the market to appeal to our rational side and to switch off our emotions, including our sense of fairness, does not make us happy. The collective outcome of the market system clashes with our individual experience of happiness. Again, there is a discrepancy between individual rationality (in this case in the sense of individual happiness) and collective rationality. The market system therefore does not necessarily lead to the greatest possible happiness for everyone.

Box 2.1. How Clever Marketing Appeals to System I

The market system may well largely appeal to our rational side, but it does not shy away from using System I if that promotes the sale of goods and services. This phenomenon plays a particularly significant role in marketing which has more to do with psychology than economics.

When I was a student, we read Vance Packard's bestseller *The Hidden Persuaders*.* The book was a detailed summary of the techniques used by these so-called hidden persuaders to get people to buy products, largely by using techniques which appeal to our emotions. At the time Sigmund Freud was still popular, so marketers attempted to map out the subconscious mind of the individual in order to appeal to their subconscious desires in advertisements.

Freud's reputation is not what it was, but marketers continue to think like psychologists and research the entire range of our emotions in order to appeal to them. When selling cars, for example, motives such as power, aggression, and even love and sex are laid on thick. When looking at car adverts the objective information is conspicuous by its absence, while the imagery sneakily appeals to all kinds of emotions.

The market system therefore also appeals to our System I. Nevertheless individuals do not achieve happiness this way. When they discover that marketers are manipulating their emotions to tempt them into buying things, it leaves them with a sour taste.

I stand by my conclusion: the market primarily appeals to System II, our rational side, and if it appeals to System I, it is instrumental, by manipulating our emotions without us always realizing it, inducing particular purchasing behaviour.

* Vance Packard, *The Hidden Persuaders* (London: Longmans, Green, 1957).

In Conclusion

The market system is an extraordinarily effective mechanism for creating material prosperity. Countries which have renounced the market system, as in the case of many previously communist regimes, have learned the hard way that it leads to stagnation and collective poverty. Capitalism, by contrast, is so successful thanks to its decentralized character, whereby everyone strives for his or her own interests.

The market system, however, also comes up against its limits, which arise because individual and collective rationality do not coincide. Firms which pollute the air and water may maximize their individual profit, but not the prosperity of society as a whole. The market system also awakens the cold, calculating System II in individuals, without taking into account our emotional side, System I, thus leading to internal conflict in individuals.

In Chapters 2 to 4 I will systematically investigate these various limits of the market system, gaining further insight into the question of why it is so unpopular with many people.

CHAPTER 3

EXTERNAL LIMITS
OF CAPITALISM

The market mechanism works well when individual and collective rationality coincide. When that is not the case, difficulties arise. Striving for individual interests in those cases does not lead to prosperity for everyone. The system comes up against its limits and will be challenged by the many who do not benefit from it or are harmed by it.

In this chapter we delve deeper into the discrepancy between individual and collective rationality, concentrating on externalities as the cause of that discrepancy. These externalities lead to external limits on the market system.

First External Limit: The Environment

Many economic activities cause externalities. If I get into the car to go shopping, my car emits toxic gases and particles into the air. Passers-by who inhale these gases suffer as a result. Their health is damaged by my decision to drive, but I do not take this into account when I decide to step into my car.

It would be different if the passers-by whose health was damaged dropped in to present me with their medical bills. I would think twice next time, perhaps cycling to the shops or simply walking to avoid such hefty fees. But since no one expects me to cover the costs, I simply continue to drive my car without considering the external costs I generate, because nothing in the system calls me to account and forces me to do so. In economists' jargon, I do not have to 'internalize' the external costs, to take them into consideration when deciding whether or not to drive somewhere.

Theoretically anyone who incurs damage from the harmful substances my car has emitted could go to court to claim damages, but it would be an extremely laborious process. After all, there are plenty of other cars driving around inflicting harm on the health of passers-by. Who is responsible for what proportion of this? Many of these passers-by also often travel by car themselves and have in turn inflicted damage on me when I walked by. It is almost impossible to establish the responsibilities for damage to health and make those responsible pay.

If we want to tackle this problem, we will need to bring in the government, which will have to compel people one way or another to control and curb the emission of harmful substances. Without such government action this will not work, a matter to which we will return later. For now it will suffice to note that the free market system has no mechanism for automatically curbing these external costs. The consequence is that individual rationality (my decision to go ahead and drive to the shops) creates collective irrationality (the damage many people suffer as a result of my individual decision). What is good for me turns out to be very bad for many others. The more people who get into the car, the stronger the discrepancy between the satisfaction of all those individual car drivers and collective well-being.

The same problem arises at the company level. Almost every company creates external costs it does not take into account when deciding whether to produce more or less. Companies emit substances which damage individuals and other companies. Here again it is very difficult to establish the individual responsibilities for the damage, and governments will have to address the problem (through prohibition or a tax on the emission of certain substances, for example).

The conclusion here is the same as in the case of the driver. Firstly, the existence of external costs means that the calculations made by individual companies to maximize their profits do not lead to the greatest possible prosperity for society as a whole. Entrepreneurs do not take into account the external costs others incur when calculating their own costs and profits. What is rational on an individual level is not necessarily rational for the community in its entirety.

Secondly, the problem can only be solved by calling in an external body to set matters in order, compelling individual actors to take into account the costs they generate. The market system does not do this automatically. It requires external control and setting boundaries. (This latter point is sometimes disputed, so we will return to it in detail in Chapter 6.)

How can these boundaries be established? There is no obvious answer. Of course we can easily point to the government, but it is not that simple. The government consists of people with access to patchy information as to the magnitude of damage, the identity of the culprits, and so on. Political authorities are also influenced by those who have caused the damage, as well as those who have suffered it. In a democracy both parties have a vote. The government, the politicians who want to be re-elected, will therefore listen to both parties and must try to reconcile their opposing interests. This is not an easy task.

The government will have to take action, but this will come in fits and starts. We can be sure of this much: the more extensive the externalities, the greater the pressure will be from those who have suffered damage to put an end to the external costs. Driven by the protests of those suffering damage, the government will be compelled to curb those who generate external costs. These curbs entail establishing limits on the working of the free market.

We therefore arrive at the following paradox. The more successful the market system is in its expansion and its capacity to create material progress (and as we have seen, it is extremely successful at this), the greater the chance that the system will come up against the boundaries set by government, which curb its freedom. The market therefore exhibits self-destructive tendencies.

This dynamic is increasingly conspicuous in a country such as China, where the extraordinary success of the market system in generating economic growth has led to the destruction of ever greater parts of the environment (air, water, nature), with alarming consequences for the health of millions of people. According to a 2007 report by the World Bank, 760,000 Chinese citizens die each year as a result of air and water pollution. The discrepancy between individual and collective rationality is greater there today than anywhere else in the world. In time the government will have to stop the rise of the free market system and subject it to controls and regulation.

Global Warming

Nowhere does the phenomenon of externalities play a greater role than in the emission of carbon dioxide (CO_2). Emission of this harmful gas creates external costs, as do other gases and chemicals. The fact that CO_2 nestles high in the atmosphere, generating external costs across borders, makes it much more difficult to achieve control over the effects.

When external costs remain geographically limited, it is easier to establish the boundaries of the market system. If the damage remains local (pollution of a river, for example), political pressure to exercise control on the companies causing the damage will be much quicker to take effect, as local residents will organize themselves politically to ensure control of companies.

The case of CO_2 emissions is different. The effects of the emissions cross borders, creating external costs outside a particular country. National politicians will hesitate to take action because every measure taken by a single national government to restrict CO_2 emissions creates advantages outside the borders, while the government which takes action is left with the entire cost. This can only be solved by international cooperation, but that is very difficult to organize, so companies and private individuals the world over continue to emit CO_2 with impunity.

Scientists have now established that CO_2 emissions are the most significant cause of global warming, although the long-term effects of that warming remain unclear. Optimists such as Björn Lomborg say that a policy of adaptation will allow us to live on a warmer planet.[3] When the sea level rises, building more dykes will suffice—problem solved. If some parts of the world become uninhabitable due to the heat, people will move to other parts which have become more habitable due to global warming.

There are, however, other, less optimistic scenarios,[4] which assume that the environmental system is non-linear. This means that tipping points can be reached at which the ecological balance is disturbed. The system might then change rapidly, with catastrophic consequences for large parts of the world. Large areas may become uninhabitable, potentially changing so quickly that people do not have time to adapt.

Climatologists have long warned that such tipping points are quite likely. A scenario often discussed by climatologists runs as follows.[5] There are large quantities of accumulated methane gas under the permafrost in Siberia. Global warming is gradually thawing this permafrost, which could at some point lead to large quantities of methane escaping into the atmosphere. Methane is far more harmful than CO_2 and might dramatically hasten global warming. This is an example of a non-linear effect.

This non-linearity is schematically reflected in Figure 3.1. The horizontal axis shows world CO_2 emissions, the vertical axis global warming. In the initial phase we see that the rise in CO_2 emissions leads to a gradual, linear temperature increase. Since the earth warms up slowly and gradually in this phase, people have time to adapt. They can build higher dykes around the land and protect the cities against the rising sea level. They can also gradually move from places where agriculture becomes unproductive due to warming to parts of the world where rising temperatures have expanded opportunities for agriculture. And they can investigate new technologies for neutralizing the effects of rising temperatures. That is the account offered by Lomborg.

When we reach tipping point A, however, there is a sudden acceleration in warming. From that point on, gradual adaptation will no

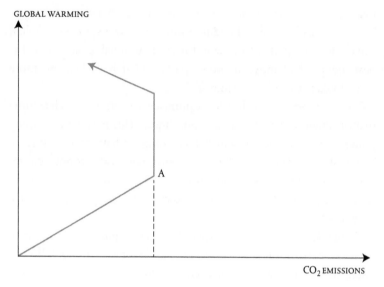

Figure 3.1. Rising temperatures and CO_2 emissions: a non-linear relationship

longer be possible. The sudden rise in temperature leads to rapid destruction of the agricultural potential of large parts of the world and there will be a shortage of drinking water in many areas.

Such catastrophic developments will inevitably lead to great conflict between countries and populations within countries. There will be serious scarcities of food, water, agricultural land, and habitable land in general. People who want to survive will start conflicts with neighbours, which in turn will lead to disruption of the economy. The markets will no longer function to ensure material prosperity, so governments will be compelled to step in and take charge.

Once we have reached point A, the market will come up hard against its limits. Governments will take over and subject the people to a dictatorship. The market system will no longer work and the economy will collapse. This will also result in emissions suddenly dropping due to reduced production. From point A, emissions (horizontal axis) will drop abruptly, but the temperature rise (vertical axis) will simply continue, at least for a while, because past emissions have a very delayed effect on global temperatures.

In his fascinating book *Collapse*, Jared Diamond has sketched out the history of civilizations, great and small, which have disappeared.[6] The best-known example is the Mayans in Middle America, who disappeared over the course of a few decades, before Columbus discovered America. The cause of this decline was overly intensive use of environmental resources such as water and wood, making them increasingly scarce. When there was a minor change in climate, the environment in which the Mayans lived was no longer capable of producing resources to sustain the population. This led to famine and wars between the different areas of the Mayan kingdom. The chaos and indiscriminate violence which ensued led to the collapse of their entire civilization in a relatively short period.

The same pattern can be observed in the collapse of other civilizations, such as Easter Island. The question is whether such scenarios can repeat themselves on a worldwide scale.* At the moment we do not know the answer. It is certain, though, that the phenomenal material growth made possible by the market system leads to growing external costs in large areas of the world. So far we have not developed a mechanism to rein in that growth, so the distance between individual and collective rationality is continually growing worldwide. There is a real danger that the market clashing with its own limits will become a more serious problem, leading to the destruction of the system.

---

* Economists have analysed similar scenarios. In the 1970s the Club of Rome published an influential report, 'The Limits to Growth', which even predicted when the collapse would take place (before the year 2000) based on an economic model. The report showed excessive trust in mathematical models for precise predictions. Since then economists have been more careful. This does not mean that non-linear scenarios such as that in Figure 3.1 are impossible, but that precise predictions are very difficult. For a recent mathematical model see Safa Motesharrei, Jorge Rivas, and Eugenia Kalnay, 'Human and nature dynamics (HANDY): Modeling inequality and use of resources in the collapse or sustainability of societies', *Ecological Economics*, 101 (May 2014), pp. 90–102 <http://www.sciencedirect.com/science/article/pii/S0921800914000615>.

Technological Optimism

As shown in the previous section, opinions on the future of our planet are largely coloured by technological optimism or pessimism. I referred to Lomborg, who is optimistic about the human capacity for adaptation to changes in temperature.

The optimists believe that the market system offers sufficient adaptive mechanisms to avoid catastrophes. For instance, if economic growth continues, the scarcity of fossil fuels will increase, causing the price of fuel to rise, in turn having a double effect. Firstly companies will use their ingenuity to develop new energy-saving technologies. Cars will become more fuel-efficient, houses better insulated, and so on. Secondly, the high price of fossil fuels will lead to a search for alternatives and renewable energy sources. An additional effect of this development is that CO_2 emissions will automatically be reduced. If global warming progresses in the meantime, we will adapt with new technologies too. In this optimistic scenario the market system will triumph and automatically solve environmental problems.

This very optimistic vision, however, overlooks two problems already mentioned. Firstly, the environmental problems are the result of external costs which companies do not take into account. That will not change automatically, without an organization outside the market compelling companies to do so. I will return to this in detail in Chapter 5. Secondly, this technological optimism is based on linear development of climate change, which is supposed to give us time to adapt. Unfortunately at this point in time it is far from clear whether the phenomenon we are dealing with is linear or non-linear. The technological pessimists generally assume that the phenomenon is non-linear, allowing us insufficient time to adapt.

The Second External Limit: The Financial Markets

While it is evident that there are externalities when it comes to the environment, this is much less clear in the case of the financial markets. Nevertheless, these also exist and cause serious problems for the market system. We were recently forced to face this fact during the 2008 banking crisis. The system suddenly reached its limits. It stood on the edge of the precipice. If there had been no government to bail out the banks at the time, we might have no market system at all in many countries by now.

Particularly since the 1980s, economists have adhered to an idealized image of financial markets, one similar to Adam Smith's view of the economy in general. When this is applied to financial markets it gives us the following narrative. Investors eager to achieve high rates of return have to collect as much information as possible to achieve their goal. Equity investors, for example, will want to know as much as possible about the companies issuing the shares. If companies are growing and are expected to continue to grow, investors will buy their shares, resulting in rising share prices for those companies and more financial resources for further growth. The financial markets are therefore efficient in that they ensure that financial savings go to companies and projects with the best chances of future success.

Furthermore, in this idealized view the financial markets are stable. Investors spread their risks and keep a check on the behaviour of those who use their money to invest, to ensure they do not take too many risks. They may exercise control either directly or indirectly, by investing in funds or financial institutions which exercise control on their behalf. In this way no one takes so much risk that it leads to bankruptcy and complete loss of their invested capital. The financial system is self-regulating.

One of the great advocates of this theory was Alan Greenspan, who was chairman of the Federal Reserve, the US central bank. His position made him one of the most powerful men in the world. He used his influence to deregulate the US financial system in the belief that the financial markets would regulate themselves, and that there was no need for government-imposed rules and regulations. He called the Wall Street bankers the 'pollinating bees' of the market system, asserting that there was absolutely no reason to put obstacles in the way of their amazing productivity.[7] Completely free financial markets would ensure that savings were used to finance the best investment projects (efficiency) and that the mechanism remained stable.

We now know better. The financial crisis which erupted in 2008 has shown that this is a fairy tale. What went wrong? It was probably a combination of many factors, the most significant being the fact that this theory did not take externalities in the financial markets into consideration. How do externalities arise in the financial markets? Here we will address that question, distinguishing between two different sources of externalities.

Herd Effects in the Financial Markets

Consumers and businesses wanting to invest must make predictions. The future, however, is dark. No one knows what will happen, even if many claim that they do. Economists in particular often give the impression that they have a crystal ball, but that is not the case. There is no science of the future, only guesses and unreliable predictions.

Nevertheless, as consumers or producers we often want to know what will happen. Since the future is dark, we look to one another, often assuming (generally erroneously) that certain people (the gurus) know what will happen in the future. When we follow them this leads to herd effects, which lead to externalities. A decision by a particular entrepreneur to invest in a new project, for example, becomes a signal to others that this entrepreneur has information about the future. Other companies follow this signal, potentially leading to a collective movement which boosts investments. This investment boom leads to optimism, encouraging even more companies to leap on the bandwagon. Euphoria follows. Banks see this happening and join in, permitting high levels of credit, leading to a boom fueled by bank credit.

Such collective movements often take place in real estate. At a certain point a collective process of optimism arises. House and building prices rise. The value of the collateral which banks generally require for a mortgage rises, so they are willing to offer more mortgages, creating a self-fulfilling prophecy. Optimism about the future of real estate leads the banks to offer more loans, further increasing prices and reinforcing that optimism.

We also see that in this mechanism the self-regulating character of the financial markets disappears. Everyone is optimistic, euphoric even. This euphoria has a blinding effect, and few people notice the risks. Real estate prices and share prices continue to rise. The markets exercise no disciplining influence whatsoever on people's behaviour. On the contrary, they lead the way to increased euphoria and an ever greater lack of discipline.

As Carmen Reinhart and Kenneth Rogoff emphasize in their book *This Time is Different*,[8] in periods of euphoria people tell tales which suggest that the price rises in shares or real estate are the result of fundamental developments. They believe that these high prices are the consequence of new technological developments and are completely justified. There is no question of a bubble.

Then comes the crash. At some point it becomes abundantly clear that the euphoria has led to inflated share and real estate prices. A correction is unavoidable. Share prices collapse and real estate prices drop substantially. Everyone who has incurred debt to buy shares or real estate suffers significant losses and can no longer afford to pay what they owe. The banks that have lent the money also encounter difficulties. A crisis breaks out, pessimism sets in, and the economy goes into recession.

The dynamics of euphoria and boom which later turn to pessimism and recession have been part and parcel of capitalism for hundreds of years, always bringing it up against its limits. These dynamics are the result of an externality. People's predictions form a collective process, with one person's expectations affecting others. These dynamics bear no resemblance to the fairy tale of the efficient market in which individuals independently gather information to make the best prediction without being influenced by others.

In this connection Keynes compared the predictions in financial markets to a beauty contest organized as follows: each jury member, instead of choosing the candidate he thinks most beautiful, chooses the girl he thinks will be branded most beautiful by the jury.

External Risk Effects in the Banking System

There is a second source of externalities in the financial markets, primarily relating to risks arising from within the banking system. Banks attempt to control their risks by setting capital aside as a buffer against possible losses on their loans, without however taking into account the risks they create outside their own institution. This externality arises because banks are interconnected, due to the fact that they loan money to one another, primarily through the interbank market. If one bank suffers a loss and fails, it takes others with it, because they have outstanding loans with the bank which initially suffered losses. The risk of each bank is therefore integral to the risk of the system as a whole.

Another characteristic of banks increases these risks still further. Banks take short-term funds (such as current accounts and savings accounts) and transform them into long-term loans (investments loans to businesses and mortgages). As long as depositors have confidence in the banking system, there is no problem. Depositors keep their money in the bank and bankers can use these short-term funds to grant long-term loans.

However, lack of confidence can arise suddenly. The scenario is almost always the same. A particular bank suffers serious losses on outstanding loans, for instance because the company receiving the loan has gone bankrupt. Depositors hurry to the bank to withdraw their money. Since the money is tied up in long-term loans, the bank cannot meet the demand and has to close. Depositors in other banks who are unsure as to whether their own banks also have bad loans opt to be on the safe side and run to their own banks. These may be in perfect order with not a single bad loan on the balance sheets, but that is irrelevant. The fear of potential bad loans is sufficient to cause a run on the bank. The house of cards collapses. Banks should take this externality into account, but generally do not.

Booms and Busts in Capitalism

The combination of herd effects and insufficient provision for external risks makes financial markets unstable. Some will say that this is no problem, or worse still, that this is a wonderful feature of capitalism, the booms and busts providing an adequate mechanism for purification. During a boom excesses arise. After the crash and downturn the system is cleansed. Those who have made the wrong decisions or taken too many risks go under, leaving behind the strong, in a form of social Darwinism.

This vision is extremely cynical, yet also naive. It is cynical because there are a great many people among the losers who have not made bad decisions nor run excessive risks, but who are dragged along in the downturn. During the banking crisis of 2008, for example, many good banks were dragged along by the wave of mistrust which arose due to the unprecedented risks taken by a few, including some of the biggest names on the market. They were punished for sins they had not committed. Social Darwinism is in any case a naive vision. After all, the losers, a great many people during a financial crisis, will not just sit idle. They call on the government to limit the damage. The market system has reached its limit. The loss of prosperity by the many who have suffered harm leads them to argue for a different mechanism of wealth distribution, the political mechanism. So we see that when the market system has reached its limit, governments become important in protecting people by restricting the market's domain.

This protection by governments can sometimes be very perverse. Large banks profit from it because they are so big that the government cannot allow them to fail as a result of the crisis. That would damage the economy too badly, because many people would be pulled into bankruptcy. Large banks are too big to fail and they know it. In fact governments provide these banks with a guarantee that they will not go bankrupt. This leads to what economists call 'moral hazard'. A large bank which enjoys implicit government insurance will therefore take more risks. These high risks lead to large profits when everything is going well, and when things go badly, governments step in and the taxpayer must cover the losses. Perversely enough, the bank's profits are privatized and its losses are nationalized. This is an unsustainable system which compels governments to step in.

This is what happened after the 2008 banking crisis. Governments were forced to help the losers (failing bankers, millions of people who became unemployed as a result of the crisis). In many countries they did this by raising spending, increasing budgetary deficits. They also forced the banking sector to introduce more regulations for risk control. This led to more regulation of the financial sector in general. The banking lobby resists this and sometimes succeeds in weakening regulations. Nevertheless the banks are now subject to significantly more checks by governments. It is unlikely that this will rule out future banking crises. Sooner or later banks will develop new techniques to take greater risks, evading the increased control of supervisors.

Third External Limit: Public Goods

Years ago my wife and I were invited to dinner with a colleague. He lived in a beautiful neighbourhood with large houses. When we arrived at his street, it turned out to be a dirt road full of potholes. We had to drive very slowly because many of the potholes were unavoidable. When we asked my colleague why his street was in such bad condition, he replied that it was a private street, belonging to the residents.

'Well,' I asked him, 'why don't you get together and pool resources to smarten up the street?'

'That's easier said than done', he replied.

Several owners preferred living on a badly maintained street to paying up, so it turned out to be impossible to put down a decent road surface. All the residents lived in magnificent houses, but the street leading to them had remained stuck in medieval times.

This incident illustrates the core problem of public goods. They are goods which benefit everyone and over which no one can exercise a private property right. These differ fundamentally from private goods such as bread, cars, books, or houses. These are goods which become my private property as soon as I buy them, enabling me to prevent others from using them. I have an exclusive right to these private goods. Ownership rights for public goods are collective. The collective may be a limited group of people, such as the residents of my colleague's street, or they may be all the residents of a country, who all enjoy national security, the prime example of a public good. The fact that ownership of a public good is collective also means that no member of the collective can be excluded from its use.

The market system has no mechanism for creating public goods. In a market individuals buy private goods and purchasers gain individual, exclusive ownership rights. We cannot buy a piece of road on which we can exercise exclusive rights. On the market we all take entirely individual decisions.

In order to buy a public good, a group of individuals must come together to make a collective decision, which in turn must lead to an agreement as to the question of how many public goods there should be (for example how many roads to build) and how the costs should be distributed. A collective decision of this kind is difficult to achieve voluntarily due to what economists call the 'free rider problem'.

The Free-Rider Problem

Imagine that a decision needs to be made as to whether a public good is to be created, perhaps a park or a road; it might also be public order and security, which can be guaranteed by police and the judiciary. Assume the principle of free participation is to be used, so advocates of the public good will have to pay and opponents will not. In that case many people will pretend to oppose the idea in order to avoid paying, while speculating that they will be able to use the public good like everybody else. The consequence of such free-riding behaviour is that too few people will contribute and the public good will never come into being, even if a large majority of people want it.

The free-rider problem involves an underlying externality. By not contributing to financing a public good, the individual creates an external effect, namely that the public good is not produced and that no one can benefit from it. Here again a discrepancy arises between private and collective rationality. Individuals who decide not to contribute (and to be free-riders) are in fact entirely rational from their perspective. After all, if the collective good comes into being, thanks to sufficient willingness among other individuals to pay for it, they will benefit because they cannot be excluded from its use. If too many individuals follow this reasoning, however, the public good will never come into being. What is rational at the individual level does not work at the collective level.

Note that individuals create an external cost which must be borne by others due to their *refusal to act* (specifically to contribute to a collectively financed public good). In the previous paragraphs we looked at situations in which individuals cause external costs by *taking action* (driving, manufacturing steel). In either case, the individuals do not take into account the external effects of their action or inaction, and it turns out that what is rational at the individual level is not rational for the collective as a whole. The fact that all individuals make the best possible decisions for themselves in this case does not lead to maximum prosperity for everyone. It is perfectly possible that even then, no one will really be satisfied with the collective result of all those decisions.

People who want public goods—and there are a whole range of public goods and services which a great many people want—will have to appeal to a mechanism other than the market. That other mechanism is government, as that is a way of achieving collective action. It will take the following form. If a majority is in favour of a particular public good (such as a park in the city), then the government will mandate that the public good should come into being. What makes this collective decision-making process special is that everyone has to contribute by paying taxes. Those who do not really want the public good will also contribute, which of course is regrettable. Force is never pleasant, but it is the only way to produce a public good.

Is there a danger that as the domain of the market grows ever greater it will supress the production of public goods? That does not necessarily have to be the case, since public goods can and generally are produced by private enterprises. Most of our roads and bridges are built by private companies, which are generally better able to do this than public enterprises. Only the decision mechanism which leads to the building of roads and bridges is collective in nature and must work via governments. The question then is whether, in a world in which the market mechanisms reach ever further, there will be a decrease in willingness to contribute to public goods and call on a collective decision mechanism.

Let us begin with a look at the facts. Figure 3.2 shows the development of the share of government investments in GDP in the eurozone since 1980. Government investments are annual expenditure by government to enable the building of roads, bridges, public buildings, harbours, and airports. We see a substantial drop in government investment in the eurozone, as well as in most other industrialized countries.

The drop in government investment coincides with the expansion of the domain of the market. It seems that there is a mechanism which ensures that as the importance of the market increases, public goods come under pressure. In Chapter 4 we will discuss what this mechanism is. It relates to the internal limits of the market. Before we can answer this important question we must first analyse these internal limits.

Finally, another parallel can be drawn here with the external environmental costs we investigated above. This analysis shows that the expansion of the market also leads to an increase in external environmental costs. In other words, the expansion of the market goes hand in hand with an increase in public harm, the demise of clean air and water, and degradation of nature. This can also be seen as a negative public good which no one can avoid. After all, we all suffer from the loss of quality of nature.

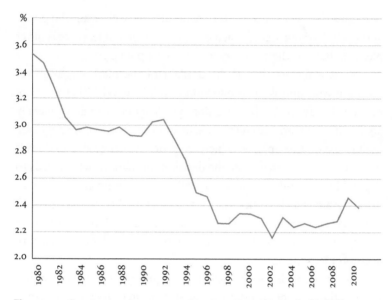

Figure 3.2. Government investments in eurozone countries (in % GDP)
Source: European Commission, AMECO database

The expansion of the markets therefore has a double effect: it leads to increasing public harm and decreasing public good. When this dynamics goes too far, the market reaches its limits and people will organize for change. They may even want to overthrow the market system.

In Conclusion

The theme of this chapter was the discrepancy between individual and collective rationality which occurs when individuals do not take into account external effects of their individual decisions. In a market system individuals have no interest in considering external effects. The problem is felt in three domains. Firstly an uncontrolled market system leads to degradation of the environment, which increases as the market system expands. A public harm is therefore created and becomes increasingly important. Secondly, the expansion of the financial markets during an economic boom also leads to public harm, namely the instability of a more risky system from which no one can escape. Thirdly, paradoxically enough, the expansion of the market leads to a decrease in interest in public goods.

Another important lesson we can draw from this chapter is that the limits of the market system are not fixed. If the market reaches its boundaries, they move, shrinking its domain. The harder the clash at the boundaries, the more significant the shrinkage. We will return to this dynamics later.

The important point we should remember is that when the market system reaches its limits, governments grow stronger, setting in motion a process aimed at restricting the markets. This applies both to financial markets and to the market system in general when it leads to environmental damage. There is therefore something self-destructive in the success of the market system.

Having read this chapter the reader might come away with the impression that I am against the market system. This could not be further from the truth. As stated, the free market is a wonderful mechanism to inspire people to take the initiative and find creative solutions to economic problems. No other system has succeeded so well in creating material prosperity. The emphasis in this chapter, however, was on the limits of the market, which need analysing in detail in order to come to greater insight as to its strengths and weaknesses. This will also bring us to a better understanding of the ideal distribution of responsibilities between market and government.

CHAPTER 4

INTERNAL LIMITS OF CAPITALISM

The market appeals to our rational side (System II) and tends to encourage us to switch off our emotions (System I), including our sense of justice, creating a tension in each of us. Our identity, after all, is not exclusively determined by the rational, calculating self. Our emotional dimension is at least as important for our individual happiness. In this chapter we investigate further how this tension between Systems I and II is stoked up by the market and thus leads to a discrepancy between individual and collective well-being. We will explore three mechanisms which lead to such a discrepancy.

First Discrepancy: Market and Distribution

I will use a very simple example to illustrate this problem, namely the market for bread. Figure 4.1 shows the relationship between supply and demand for bread. Demand is indicated by the declining line, representing the phenomenon whereby falling prices lead to greater willingness among consumers to buy a loaf of bread. We also assume there are hundred potential bread buyers.

Supply is indicated by the rising line. The upward movement reflects the phenomenon whereby when the price of bread rises it becomes attractive to bakers to bake more bread (not because they like the consumers, but because they can make more profit by producing more when the price increases).

A price is set at point E, where demand is equal to supply. Economists call this the equilibrium point and the resulting price the equilibrium price. In our example this is 2 pounds. At this price fifty people will buy a loaf of bread. (We assume here that each buyer buys just one loaf, although this hypothesis has no bearing on our conclusion.)

We now note the following:

- Firstly, some of the fifty people who bought a loaf of bread for 2 pounds would also be prepared to pay more. If the price were 3 pounds, some of them would drop out, reducing demand, but there would still be a group willing to pay 3 pounds or more.
- Secondly, the fifty people who do not buy bread (consumers between 50 and 100 on the horizontal axis) consider 2 pounds too high a price. They therefore do not buy bread.

The traditional economists' interpretation of this result is as follows. The fifty consumers who buy bread for 2 pounds are those who attach a high value to bread. The fifty consumers who do not are those who attach less value to bread. In this traditional economic analysis the free market leads to the optimal solution, ensuring that bread reaches those who care the most about it, and who are prepared to pay the most. It is good that bread reaches those who most want it; in other words, those most willing to pay.

But willingness to pay is just one possible interpretation of the difference between the first fifty consumers and the second fifty. This was Marie-Antoinette's interpretation when told that the Parisians were protesting at the high price of bread. Her response, 'Let them eat cake', suggests there is indeed nothing wrong with the market system. If the second group of people in Figure 4.1 do not want bread, they should eat cake instead.

Assume, however, that the second group consists of people who are ill or disabled and have no income. They may well attach great value to bread and might be willing to buy it, but 2 pounds is too much. They lack the financial means to buy bread at that price. In a free market system this leads to exactly the same equilibrium. The market is completely indifferent to the underlying reason why the second group does not buy bread. Whether it is because they do not

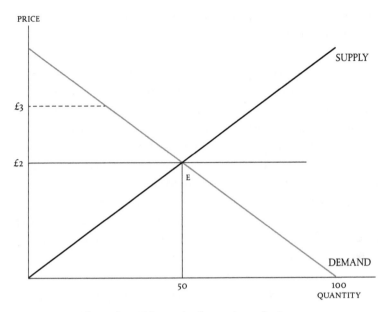

PRICE

£3

£2

E

SUPPLY

DEMAND

50

100
QUANTITY

Figure 4.1. Bread supply and demand: who receives what?

want bread and prefer cake or because they cannot afford it, it makes no difference to the equilibrium which arises in a free market.

Can we then conclude that the result of the free market, namely that fifty people buy loaves of bread for 2 pounds apiece and fifty do not, is socially optimal? The answer for any person with common sense can only be no. It is sometimes disturbing to note how many economists lack such common sense and continue to insist that an equilibrium such as that in Figure 4.1 is optimal. It is certainly not optimal for the group of fifty who do not buy bread and go hungry. Nor is it optimal for the first group of fifty who do buy bread. Why not?

This first group consists of individuals subject to Systems I and II. System II might tell them that the market result is just fine and maximizes their individual benefit. System I, however, regulates our emotions, including our sense of fairness. There are individuals in group I (not all of them, of course) who will be unhappy because

41

the result contravenes their sense of justice. Some might even share their bread with the poor.

The free market will not solve this problem. It will have to be tackled some other way. A possible solution is individual charity, but that will not normally be sufficient. This will need to be supplemented by government action, which can be stimulated by the second group protesting against the inequality in bread distribution.

In actual fact the production and distribution of bread illustrates external as well as internal limits to a free market system. The external limit is the fact that a significant proportion of the population does not achieve satisfaction in such a system. What is optimal for part of the population is not optimal for society as a whole. The segment left dissatisfied may revolt and use the government route to force a different result from that of the market.

The internal limit of the free market is reached here because some of the individuals from the first group are also unhappy. These are the individuals whose sense of fairness is offended. Some will make efforts to achieve a fairer distribution of bread via political channels. The market reaches its limits because it comes up against a feeling in many individuals that the system is unfair. A number of those

---

Box 4.1. Development of World Inequality

Worldwide we observe two phenomena. Firstly we see that in a number of countries, especially in Asia, average incomes are rising rapidly. As a consequence inequality between the industrialized countries and the rapidly growing economies is decreasing. Africa remains a big exception, although over the past decade incomes in Africa have begun to rise.

A second phenomenon is that inequality within countries is on the rise almost everywhere. In some parts of the world, especially the Anglo-Saxon countries, the rise in inequality since the 1980s, when liberalization rose sharply, has been particularly spectacular. In Figure 4.2 we see that since 1980 the share held by the top ten per

cent in income distribution in these countries has increased dramatically.* The inequality reached in these countries in 2010 is comparable with that of the early 1930s, just before the Great Depression.

In many fast-growing Asian economies we see the same phenomenon: a sharp rise in income inequality. This has continued
since the liberalization of the economy.

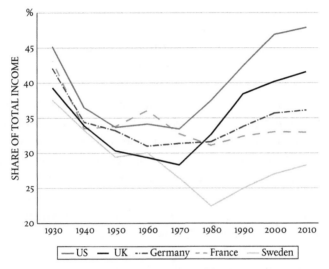

Figure 4.2. Share of total income received by top 10% in Western
countries

Source: <http://topincomes.g-mond.parisschoolofeconomics.eu/#Database>

A number of continental European countries have undergone a
less pronounced increase in inequality, also shown in figure 4.2.
Inequality dropped steadily from the 1930s until the start of the
1980s. In Germany and Sweden we see a significant rise since then,
but less so in France.

Is there a law of modern capitalism which causes inequality to
rise continually? This appears to be the case in Anglo-Saxon and
Asian countries. It is less clear in continental Europe. Some people,
including Thomas Piketty of the Paris School of Economics, believe
that global capitalism does indeed lead to increasing inequality. We
will return to this theory in detail in Chapter 12.

---

* There are many other measures of inequality. The frequently used Gini
coefficient also points to a sharp rise in inequality in these countries.

individuals will decide to take action to change the free market system. We have often seen this phenomenon in history. Individuals from the materially wealthier classes cannot live with distribution in a market system (e.g. Karl Marx, Friedrich Engels, Lenin) and take action, mobilizing the people in the lowest income groups. In the past this has led to protests and revolutions which have brought violent change to the market system.

Second Discrepancy: Intrinsic and Extrinsic Motivation

Psychologists talk about intrinsic and extrinsic motivation. Intrinsic motivation means that people are motivated to put effort into their work or other activities because they are fulfilled by the work or activity itself, as in the case of an artist receiving creative fulfilment from painting. Similarly a top manager in a position to determine business strategy might enjoy the power. People who engage in such activities are generally strongly intrinsically motivated to do their jobs well. The activity itself gives their lives meaning.

Motivation can also be extrinsic. By this term psychologists mean that people make an effort for the sake of the financial reward for a particular activity. The activity itself may not be particularly satisfying, but the reward motivates the practitioner to put in effort all the same.

In reality intrinsic and extrinsic motivation are often found together. The top manager who has an interesting job is also very well paid. Nevertheless we can formulate a number of generalizations as to the way in which the two forms of motivation are used in a market system, where a great deal of weight is given to extrinsic motivation. The system of remuneration for labour rests on extrinsic motivation. People carrying out physical or mental work are remunerated on the basis of their performance. In the ideal free market an employee is paid exclusively for his contribution to the firm's productivity. A very productive worker—someone with a significant effect on productivity—is paid more, and a less productive worker is paid less. The entire logic of a market system is based on this idea of performance in terms of productivity.

The implication is that a free market system appeals mainly to the calculating, rational System II in each of us. As individuals we are called on to exert ourselves and to achieve. Our calculating side will determine the effort proportional to the reward we receive and the way it weighs up against the costs. If the reward is high enough, we will be prepared to put in extra effort. If that is not the case, we will do less.

Now the question is whether the expansion of the domain of the free market causes the extrinsic motivation increasingly to gain the upper hand at the cost of intrinsic motivation. If that is the case, our System I is gradually suppressed and we will not feel so happy in such a market system. In that case we experience a lack of purpose in our work and our lives.

There are two schools of thought on this, the first supported mainly by non-economists, the second by economists. The first is well represented by Michael Sandel, a Harvard University philosopher who has written several perceptive books on the ethics of markets. One of Sandel's most popular titles is *What Money Can't Buy: The Moral Limits of Markets*,[9] which argues that the growing domain of the market suppresses intrinsic motivation and increasingly compels people to focus on financial incentives. He gives the example of donating blood. Many people are prepared to give blood for intrinsic reasons, and do so free of charge. In doing this, donors make it clear that their motivation lies in giving blood itself as an act of solidarity.

In the US the market mechanism has been introduced to blood donation. People who give blood receive financial compensation. The effect has been to put off many people who previously gave blood free of charge. These people feel that the financial reward removes an essential aspect of donating blood, showing solidarity with sick people. So they drop out.* This is an example in which the introduction

---

* Another effect of commercializing blood donation has been a drop in the quality of blood, since the blood donors now tend to come from lower income groups, people who

of financial incentives corrupts the nature of the act. Financial reward, an extrinsic motive, suppresses the sense of responsibility.

The other school states that the triumph of the market does not necessarily lead to suppression of intrinsic motivation. A representative of this school is Kenneth Arrow, winner of the Nobel Prize in Economics in 1972. In his view both motivations can coexist in a market system.[10]

Take the example of art. Today market mechanisms play a large role, perhaps the most significant role in the market for paintings. Top painters such as Luc Tuymans are millionaires. The extrinsic motivation to work as an artist is exceptionally high, but this does not necessarily mean that the intrinsic motivation is suppressed. The market works as a selection mechanism. An artist driven exclusively by creative fulfilment (intrinsic motivation) is free to pursue his work, and if he inspires others, he also receives market recognition. People will show a willingness to pay for his paintings. The artist will be substantially remunerated even if the financial reward is not what drives him at all.

Another example is business management. Many managers understand that to motivate employees to work hard it is not enough to offer financial incentives. Employees look for purpose and fulfilment in their work. A manager who succeeds in supplying these will enjoy greater business success, delivering greater productivity and higher profits. In other words, when employees are both intrinsically and extrinsically motivated in their work, they perform better, which ends up being better for the company. There is no contradiction between the market system and intrinsic motivation. Extrinsic motivation need not suppress intrinsic motivation.

These are two diametrically opposed ideas. How can we reconcile them? Here is an attempt. In market systems we often see mechanisms arise to reconcile intrinsic and extrinsic motivation (Systems I and II),

really need the money they receive for their blood. Unfortunately these are also people who are less healthy due to poverty.

for instance in companies which arrange their work so that people can take pleasure in it. The same applies to the arts when art lovers recognize an artist's genius, even if that artist does not care about money.

These mechanisms, however, do not always function well. Problems arise in connection with phenomena discussed in Chapter 3. Financial markets often create bubbles. The same is true of art, and essentially for the same reason. It is difficult to estimate the value of a painting (as it is difficult to predict the future). Art buyers therefore often look to others for guidance, such as art lovers, collectors, and gurus. This can lead to a collective process in which one artist or school receives an unusual level of attention. An art bubble arises, with enormous sums spent on a particular artist or movement, only to burst as suddenly as it formed.

Interest in the British artist Damien Hirst is an example of one such bubble. Hirst is famous for installations involving aquariums preserving dead animals such as cows, sheep, and sharks in formaldehyde. His shark installation was bought by a hedge fund for more than nine million euros. In 2010 *The Sunday Times* estimated Hirst's fortune at 215 million pounds—not as rich as Bill Gates, but clearly the prospect of such financial gains opens up the possibility that the art market will attract artists driven mainly by commercial, extrinsic motives.

Problems also arise in companies which wish to allow space for intrinsic motivation of staff as well as extrinsic motivation. The enormous rise in the importance of financial markets has fundamentally changed business. Companies wanting to grow are eventually obliged to float on the stock market and find it increasingly difficult to reconcile the two types of motivation. Why is that?

Among publicly listed companies there is a great pressure to produce short-term returns. After all, investors who buy shares are not entering into a long-term contract with the company. They keep the share as long as they judge that the company will remain profitable in the future. At the slightest hint of danger or doubt as to the future, they will sell their shares and prices will fall. Everything is focused on quarterly figures which the company is obliged to publish, just as politicians are constantly thinking of the next election. This leads to short-termism in business.

This short-term thinking is further reinforced by the manner in which top management is remunerated, which is increasingly based on the movements of company share prices. If the share price rises, top managers receive bonuses. They will do anything to ensure that this happens, pushing up their income. Poor quarterly results must be avoided under this reward structure, regardless of the cost, because they tend to have a negative influence on share prices. As a result, the entire company management is dominated by short-term movements in share prices.

The consequence is that a drop in share prices pushes top management into reorganization of the firm. Workers are fired, costs decline and profits rise. Top managers thus earn their bonus precisely at the moment when they sack lots of employees.

In this kind of environment it is very difficult to strike a balance between intrinsic and extrinsic staff motivation. Intrinsic motivation is particularly difficult to achieve when there is a permanent threat of redundancy. It is also easier for the company to focus mainly on extrinsic motivation, for instance in the form of a bonus. This can easily be cut if things do not go according to plan.

In time this may well lead to well-paid employees, but they will be less and less happy in their work. The market system in this case promotes the calculating, rational side of employees at the cost of their emotional side. A discrepancy arises between individual and collective well-being. The economy may flourish, but individuals do not feel good. The market system creates its own enemies.

Third Discrepancy: Competition and Cooperation

The free market system attaches great importance to competition. It is competition which compels companies to keep their prices low, benefiting consumers. Without competition, companies would not hesitate to raise their prices at the expense of consumer well-being. So competition is a good thing. It is also the reason why the market system has positive effects on well-being.

Nevertheless there is a paradoxical side to all this. Let us take a moment to look around us. There are many markets in which people sign contracts to deal in goods and services. At the same time we see many people working in collaboration. A company is a collaborative venture. There are millions of companies, many more than there are markets. This means that a great many economic decisions are made outside the market, within companies in which cooperation is the rule, not competition.

Why do we see so many cooperative relationships within companies? One answer is offered by British economist Ronald Coase, who won the Nobel Prize in Economics in 1991. His answer was as follows. Market transactions lead to transaction costs. The buyers and sellers have to find and trust one another. Contracts must be drawn up and the quality of goods and services evaluated. If contractual terms are not met, action must be taken. All this creates transaction costs. A partnership within one and the same company can reduce or even eliminate a number of these costs.[11] Thus companies are formed which arrange a number of transactions internally. Only those transactions which can be dealt with more easily—i.e. at lower cost—take place there.

This is an attractive theory. In my view, however, it is not sufficient to explain the degree of cooperation in the economy. Coase assumes that cooperation is always the result of rational decisions by individuals, who offset the costs and benefits of collaboration. If the benefits outweigh the costs, they work together. If that is not the case, the parties go their separate ways.

The same vision was the foundation of Jean-Jacques Rousseau's social contract. According to this view we entered the world as individuals. In order to survive we draw up a partnership contract with others, leading to cooperation. Initially the individual was all alone, and only later came to the insight that cooperation sometimes offers advantages.

This, however, is not the way in which humanity evolved. The first human beings were social animals who cooperated intensely *before* they developed self-awareness, just as we see in primates today.[12] Collaboration is ingrained in all of us, and is not in the first instance the result of a rational decision by individuals who started out living alone and have now decided to work together. Cooperation was already in place *before* we became human.[†]

Many people like to cooperate and derive a great sense of fulfilment from it. Working together is fun and makes us happy. Companies exist because of a drive to work with others.

Of course competition remains important too. A company is a symbiosis of two phenomena: competition and cooperation. It is an institution which organizes the cooperation that fulfils us while also making us more resilient to competition with the outside world, an extraordinary construct.

The question is whether the rise of the free market system unbalances the relationship between cooperation and competition within a company. That does not have to be the case. Nevertheless we see that the cooperative dimension can suffer from the pressure of financial markets, which expect constant positive results. Many market-listed companies reorganize themselves into competing divisions which must each prove their profitability. The competition model existing outside companies is increasingly employed internally as well.

This tendency destroys a balance within each individual. We may each be prepared to compete with others as individuals. Many people enjoy a bit of competition, but as individuals we also have a need for cooperation. Once again the market system reaches limits within individuals. If the market compels us to see everyone as a competitor, we are hardly likely to be completely happy about this. We are all

---

[†] Of course it might be argued that collaboration is evolutionarily selected because it offers an advantage in a world of competition for scarce resources. So although it is not the result of a premeditated, conscious, and rational choice, it can be interpreted retrospectively as such.

also social creatures who find fulfilment in cooperation as well as competition.

Competition and cooperation, two sources of motivation for every human being, do not divide along the same lines as Systems I and II. As we have seen, the rational System II can also drive us to cooperate. Nevertheless the intrinsic joy of working together belongs more with the emotional System I. The success of the market system again leads to internal tension. Once again a discrepancy arises between individual and collective well-being.

Why Does Interest in Public Goods Decrease?

In Chapter 3 we noted that since the 1980s the share of public invest-ment as a proportion of GDP has fallen sharply, making less and less resources available for public goods. We see this on many levels. The quality of our roads is dropping. In Leuven, the city where I used to teach, the deep potholes in the road surfaces are barely repaired anymore. When I am in that historic city I ride a mountain bike to cope with the deep potholes and bumps disfiguring the streets. In many countries rail infrastructure is ageing, with insufficient invest-ment in replacements, resulting in failures, faults, and delays.

In this chapter we have provided a conceptual framework which enables us to understand this better. The expansion of the market system encourages individual rationality in each of us, weakening the drive for cooperation. A sort of repressive effect occurs, as the market regards us as individuals. This prompts each of us to act individually. Cooperative behaviour is not rewarded in the same way, so many of us will suppress this behaviour. However, it is a cooperative attitude which is needed to come to collective decisions which make public goods possible. The more individualized the reward system, the less space there is for cooperation, leading to an individualistic culture in which less and less importance is given to collaboration and public goods.

Over time, however, this trend is penalized. People have a need for public goods such as infrastructure, public order, and security. If they

Box 4.2. Why I Am sometimes Exasperated by Eurostar

Since February 2012 I have been teaching at the London School of Economics and have become an intense user of Eurostar's services. I travel back and forth between London and Brussels almost every week. My feelings about Eurostar are very mixed. On the one hand I appreciate the convenience and comfort with which I race through the Channel each week, arriving at my destination in the minimum time. On the other hand I curse Eurostar each month when ordering my tickets on their website. Why?

Eurostar applies the principle of price discrimination. This is a technique which companies with a monopoly apply to maximize their profits, consisting of looking at signals which betray consumers' willingness to pay. Airlines apply the same method. The greater the willingness to pay, the higher the price the company will charge. In many cases, however, it is difficult or even impossible to ascertain an individual's willingness to pay. Companies then charge everyone the same price. In the case of Eurostar (and airlines) customers do give indications of their willingness to pay. Someone buying a Eurostar ticket for the following day is probably not a tourist or a student. This is much more likely to be a business person who absolutely has to be in London the following day, enough of a signal for Eurostar to decide that this person is prepared (or compelled by circumstances) to pay a great deal for a ticket. So they charge the maximum fare. This means the price of a single ticket from Brussels to London in economy class for the next day (in fact for every day of the following week) can rise to more than 150 euros. If you are patient, however, and order a ticket for a journey a month or more in advance, Eurostar decides you are probably a tourist or student with less willingness to pay, and all they charge is 44 euros.

Of course I try to book my tickets a month or two in advance as far as possible to benefit from the much better rates, but often that is impossible because I do not know the date of my journey.

Why am I telling this story? Well, once again it is a question of Systems I and II. I understand the logic of a company like Eurostar aiming to maximize profits, squeezing customers for every cent and therefore setting the price according to willingness to pay (System II), but at the same time I am infuriated each time I do not know my journey dates far enough in advance and am lumbered with a hefty fare. I feel cheated for two reasons: firstly because I myself have signalled to Eurostar that I am prepared to pay more by ordering just before I travel; and secondly because I have to pay so much more than others for exactly the same service. System I stirs up my feelings of rage and powerlessness.

So I am simultaneously pleased with Eurostar and furious at the discriminatory way the company treats me. The more companies try to 'catch out' customers the way Eurostar does, the greater the hostility towards them. From a rational economic perspective what Eurostar does is understandable, but that rational approach runs into limits which spring from System I, leaving people feeling angry because they feel duped or discriminated against.

no longer enjoy these public goods they will overthrow a system which fails to fulfil their wishes.

In Conclusion

In this chapter we have seen how the expansion of the market system brings it to its internal limits. These relate to the fact that the market system appeals to the rational, calculating capacities of individuals, responding to financial stimuli and competition. When the free market system grows in importance, as has been the case over the last three decades, these capacities in all individuals become more important. They increasingly become standards of individual success. However, that also means that other, equally important individual characteristics which belong to the emotional System I are suppressed. These individual qualities count less and less towards determining success. For many people who care about fair income distribution, intrinsic motivation, and cooperation, this leads to a lack of fulfilment. The market system produces great material prosperity, but many people are dissatisfied all the same, because individual happiness is not achieved, or is even repressed. A discrepancy arises between individual and collective well-being, which can in turn lead to the rejection of the system, which is felt to be hard, cold, and unfair. If this happens the social consensus in favour of the free market system is undermined.

CHAPTER 5

THE UTOPIA OF SELF-REGULATION IN THE MARKET SYSTEM

The reader may have detected some pessimism in the previous chapters. It seems inevitable that the market system will come up against its limits, with all the consequences that entails. But are there no mechanisms within the market system itself to prevent this inevitable slide into catastrophe? It is an important question. It is also a question of the market's ability to regulate itself.

In this chapter we will explore three possible internal regulators. The first relates to the capacity of free markets to internalize external costs, the second to technological progress, and the third to saturation effects.

Can Markets Regulate Themselves?

We already came across the idea of a self-regulating market when we talked about financial markets. The idea has rather lost its sheen since the financial crisis, but remains popular among market fundamentalists, who state that the self-regulating character will ensure that the market system finds a stable equilibrium. Let us take the example of the environment. We have argued that businesses which emit harmful substances do not take into account the external costs they create. This leads them to produce excessive pollutants, with negative effects for the environment, thus creating a 'public bad' which no one can avoid.

The market fundamentalists' reply to this accusation is that the cause of the problem lies in lack of clarity in property rights. Since air and water are freely available goods, they are seen as big rubbish tips where everyone can freely dump harmful chemicals. It would therefore be sufficient to establish ownership rights over air and water. If my piece of air and pool of water is polluted, I can turn to those who have caused the damage and demand compensation. The clever market fundamentalist will also conclude that the problem lies in a lack of market. If there were a properly functioning market for air and water to which everyone had property rights, then there would be no environmental problems.[*]

That is true, of course, but it is also extremely theoretical. How will we establish those ownership rights? This is an incredibly complex information problem. How far does my ownership right over air and water extend? If the right is infringed, who is guilty? There are literally millions of people around the world who have inflicted damage on me. Where are they? Will the court in London to which I turn to enforce my rights be able to solve the information problem? And what about the billions of people who have all been harmed by billions of others? How will they account for their damage?

But even if we can solve this information problem, we run into a contradiction. In the end it will be institutions outside the market which establish and enforce these ownership rights. It can only come from government. Firstly parliament (hopefully not a dictator) will have to enshrine those property rights in law. Secondly other institutions, the courts and the police, will have to be able to enforce those rights.

Some diehard market fundamentalists will object that everything can be arranged by voluntary agreements. I come to an agreement with a few billion people to compensate them for the damage I have caused and vice versa. Everyone negotiates with everyone else, because

---

[*] This idea has been around a long time. Its origin is to be found in the famous Coase theorem which says that when property rights are properly defined an efficient outcome will emerge in which the cost of externalities will be paid by one of the parties in the contract.

in a globalized world more or less everyone generates external costs. The costs of these negotiations, however, are so high that this solution cannot be taken seriously. We have to delegate these negotiations to specialists, namely politicians.

There is no way around it. Government institutions will have to step in and apply restrictions to the market system.

Technological Progress

In Chapter 4 we referred to the possibility that the market system might succeed in reducing the use of scarce resources and energy through technological progress. We then saw that this technological progress is driven by the fact that in a growing economy the price of resources and energy increases, forming a financial incentive to look for technologies to reduce usage. I emphasized that this mechanism is absent when it comes to pollution. In the market system nothing prevents companies and consumers from generating external costs unless the government puts a stop to it. In other words, there is no internal regulator for the environment to put pressure on external costs. That regulator must come from outside the market system and can only be organized by the government.

Technological progress, however, may be able to offer some relief. Digital technologies create unprecedented possibilities for increased productivity. This is strongly emphasized in Erik Brynjolfsson and Andrew McAfee's recent book.[13] These authors see almost infinite new possibilities, which can also be used to tackle pollution.

That is a very optimistic vision of the future: new technologies will save us from our downfall. If that is true, we are still left with the question I posed in Chapter 4, namely whether those technological revolutions will offer alternatives in time. Global warming continues unabated. Will the new technologies be ready fast enough to stop the emission of CO_2? That currently seems very doubtful.

There is also a paradox that has been investigated by Robert Gordon of the University of Wisconsin. He comes to the conclusion that

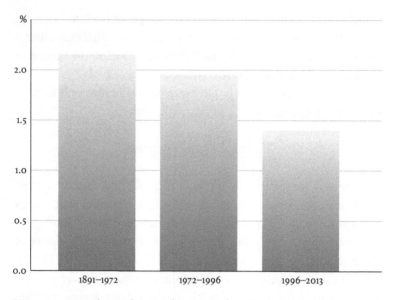

Figure 5.1. Annual growth in production per hour in the US (in %)

Source: Robert Gordon, 'The Demise of US Economic Growth: Restatement, Rebuttal, and Reflections', NBER Working Paper 19895 (February 2014)

although the digital revolution is important, it is less so than previous technological revolutions, the railways, telegraphy and telephony, the car, and air travel. These technological revolutions were at least as intrusive as the digital revolution, if not more so. They changed people's lives more extensively, and according to Robert Gordon, had a larger effect on growth in productivity than the digital revolution of the 1990s.[†]

Figure 5.1 illustrates some aspects of this, showing average annual growth in productivity (production per hour of labour) in the US since 1891. It is worth noting that the growth in productivity between 1891 and 1990 was around two per cent per year. Since then growth has dropped to less than 1.5 per cent per year. So far the digital revolution

---

[†] See Robert Gordon's fascinating recent book, *The Rise and Fall of American Growth: The US Standard of Living since the Civil War* (Princeton, NJ: Princeton University Press, 2016).

of the 1990s has had remarkably little observable effect on growth in productivity in the country where it began. This has led Robert Solow, the great American economist who won the Nobel Prize for his contribution to the theory of economic growth, to the conclusion that the new technologies are visible everywhere except in productivity growth statistics.

We see a similar trend in other developed countries, including those of the EU, as represented in Figure 5.2. This is based on Thomas Piketty's authoritative book *Capital in the Twenty-First Century*, which I will discuss in Chapter 12. Figure 5.2 shows the development of production per capita since the industrial revolution. These figures are not directly comparable with those of Figure 5.1, showing production per hour, which is a better measure of productivity. Production per capita (Figure 5.2) is also influenced by working hours.

We can see that since the 1990s growth in annual per capita productivity has slowed in Western Europe and North America.[‡]

It seems that we are returning to the 'normal' growth figures of the nineteenth century. Figure 5.2 also shows that the high growth in per capita production in the post-war period is an exception in the long history of growth.

It therefore looks as if the digital revolution has not yet succeeded in raising productivity. Of course it is the case that there is a long lead time between the development of new technology and its application in large parts of the economy. New technologies run into resistance of various kinds. There are psychological sources of resistance: people who work with old technologies will not always switch to new ones because the change means part of their knowledge has become worthless. There are also economic sources of resistance: old machines and tools have to be disposed of early, factories have to be closed down and employees sacked. This leads to serious opposition

---

[‡] This is not the case in Asian countries such as China, where we see very high growth in productivity. This is because these countries are catching up historically, which enables them to introduce Western technologies on a grand scale without having to develop them themselves.

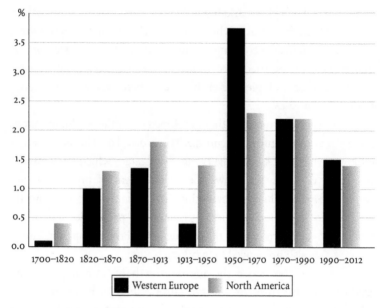

Figure 5.2. Growth production per capita since the industrial revolution (in %)

Source: Thomas Piketty, *Capital in the Twenty-First Century* (Cambridge, MA: Harvard University Press, 2014)

and delays to the introduction of new technologies. Finally it also takes a great deal of time to find applications for a new technology. True as all that is, it remains remarkable that after the outbreak of the digital revolution productivity growth is lower than in the previous fifty years. It is not so obvious that the digital revolution will provide us with the means to stop pollution.

Growth and Saturation

In 1930 John Maynard Keynes wrote a remarkable essay entitled 'Economic possibilities for our grandchildren', in which he argued that capitalism would be able to meet all of people's material needs by around 2015 (i.e. by now) due to development of productivity.

People would arrive at the insight that non-material needs were more important than material needs and would work only five to ten hours per week, leaving them able to fully enjoy leisure, art, and culture. Capitalism would therefore reach a state of internal self-regulation which would push people to satisfy their emotional and spiritual needs once their material needs were met.

In their recent book *How Much is Enough?*, the Skidelsky father and son duo return to Keynes's idea.[14] They assume that what makes people happy is the 'good life', a concept developed by the Greek philosopher Aristotle. The core of the idea is that we can only be happy if we lead a good life in which we are able to develop fully as human beings. We achieve this through intellectual and artistic activities in an environment of tolerance and friendship. Of course these activities are only possible if our material needs are met. Once that is the case, non-material needs become the priority.

This vision of the development of human needs contains a built-in curb on material growth. As material prosperity increases people look for happiness in the satisfaction of non-material needs. This dynamics ensures that the drive for increasing material production drops, relieving pressure on the environment. Capitalism automatically leads to saturation for material goods and is therefore self-regulating.

The Skidelskys, however, are forced to observe that this dream of the good life has not worked out. The development of capitalism has not yet reduced the drive to possess ever more material goods. The promise that capitalism would automatically lead to satisfaction of non-material needs has not yet been fulfilled. This comes down to two phenomena.

Firstly the dynamics of capitalism are based on a continual quest for new products. Ten years ago there were no smartphones. No one really needed a smartphone, simply because no one could imagine such a thing. Now that they exist, the pressure to have one is irresistible, as is the case with many new products. Who these days does not want a tablet, a car with the latest electronic gadgets, or a smart TV? I am sure that if Keynes were alive today he would not be averse to all these gadgets. By continually developing new, exciting products, capitalism shifts the saturation point for the satisfaction of material needs.

Secondly, even if Europeans and Americans were to strive en masse for the satisfaction of non-material needs, this would not stop the rest of the world (another six billion people) from striving for material progress. Material prosperity among those six billion people remains very meagre. For them improvement in this aspect of their lives remains the first priority.

At this moment consumption per capita in the American population is around seven times that in China. This means that the Chinese will continue to attempt to raise their material consumption for a long time to come. There are a great many unfulfilled material desires in the largest segment of the world's population. Nothing will convince them that it is better to strive for the satisfaction of non-material needs. The drive of so many people to reach the consumption levels of the Western world cannot be stopped.

It will therefore be a very long time before the internal regulator will guide the system from the satisfaction of material requirements towards non-material needs. Meanwhile the market system sails inevitably towards its limits.

Kuznets's Dream

Based on a statistical analysis of US tax data between 1914 and 1948, the American economist Simon Kuznets came to the remarkable conclusion in 1953 that income inequality in the US had dropped substantially. Based on this fact, Kuznets decided that capitalism contains a law which ensures that as a country becomes richer, income inequality drops. He expressed this in what would later be called the Kuznets curve, as shown in Figure 5.3. The horizontal axis represents income per capita, the vertical axis income inequality. We can see that when income per capita rises, inequality initially rises. Once a certain level of wealth is achieved, income inequality begins to fall.

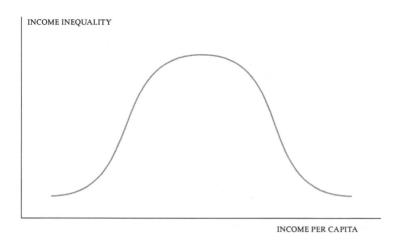

INCOME INEQUALITY

INCOME PER CAPITA

Figure 5.3. The Kuznets curve

The Kuznets curve had a great influence on generations of econo-mists and policy makers, debunking the Marxist idea that capitalism would lead to increasing inequality. This optimistic theory implied that as capitalism developed it would lose the unattractive feature of income inequality and become more socially acceptable. According to Kuznets, a self-regulating mechanism ensured that capitalism would not lead to revolutionary developments, as Marx had predicted.

In retrospect it seems that Kuznets's vision was just a dream, based on a very limited period of history, between the two world wars. During this period income inequality did indeed drop in many Western coun-tries, as shown in Figure 4.2. This drop in income inequality had a great deal to do with the revolutionary circumstances evoked by the wars, which weakened the position of the highest income earners in many countries. This was also expressed in spectacular rises in taxes on the highest incomes, as mentioned in Chapter 1.

The empirical evidence collected since then by economists such as Atkinson, Piketty, Saez, and others point to increased income inequality since the 1980s.[15] This was also illustrated in Figure 4.2 and is particularly true of the Anglo-Saxon countries. Piketty recently investigated the reasons for this trend. We will discuss his theory in Chapter 12. Here it is sufficient to conclude that no self-regulating mechanism exists in capitalism to reduce income inequality and prevent the system from clashing violently with its limits.

In Conclusion

In this chapter we questioned whether the market contains self-regulating processes which can prevent the system from ending in self-destruction. We observed that there was no in-built mechanism which can internalize the external costs created by the market system. Only an external organization, the government, can do this.

Capitalism itself is not capable of preventing an inevitable clash with its limits. Technological revolutions, in particular the digital revolution, do not currently raise productivity sufficiently to generate the resources needed to prevent environmental decline. Kuznets has turned out to be wrong in his belief that a highly developed capitalism would cause income inequality to drop. Piketty, Saez, and Atkinson point out that inequality in the most developed capitalist countries has recently increased.

The regulatory mechanisms must therefore come from outside the market system, and indeed from the government. How this should be achieved and how government regulation in turn hits its limits are the themes of Chapters 6 to 8.

CHAPTER 6

WHO CAN SAVE THE MARKET SYSTEM FROM DESTRUCTION?

In the previous chapters we argued that if the market system were left to its own devices, it would hit its limits. This clash might lead to the system sustaining serious damage, if it is not destroyed completely. I also argued that within the market system no self-regulating mechanisms exist to prevent this clash. The question then is whether there are mechanisms *outside* the market system to curb this destructive trend and thus prevent its downfall.

In this chapter we will see that in principle such a mechanism exists, made possible by government policy. We will begin by developing the theory that constitutes the foundation of the role of government as a regulator of the market system. We will also discuss three domains in which the government has a role to play: in tackling externalities, supplying public goods, and redistribution.

The Role of Governments: Externalities

Economists have developed an important theory on the question of how governments should tackle externalities. The originator of this theory was Arthur Cecil Pigou, an English economist of the first half of the twentieth century. He argued that if a company generates external costs by emitting harmful substances, the government should determine the magnitude of the costs and impose them on the company. This is best achieved by levying taxes.

Of course, once again, we run into an information problem. How can the government estimate the external damage caused by one individual company? As I argued previously, this is extremely difficult. Governments can, however, work on a trial-and-error basis. Initially a tax is imposed, for example five pounds per tonne of sulphur emissions, and the effect is measured afterwards. If sulphur emissions fall insufficiently, the tax is raised until we approach the optimal tax rate, that which ensures that sulphur emissions are so low that they no longer pose a risk to health.

Pigou also distinguished between positive and negative externalities. Negative externalities cause harm which must be tackled by government through taxes. There are also positive external effects. The classic example is renovation of house facades in the city. This brightens up the street, benefiting others beyond the house owner. Governments can encourage such activities with positive external effects by providing subsidies for renovations.

Here it is interesting to consider whether the emission of harmful substances should be fought using taxes or rather using quantitative limits on emissions (as the European system of emission standards attempts to do). Taxation is an indirect method, quantitative restrictions a direct one. Economists have been weighing up which approach is the most efficient.

The answer is not immediately clear and has led to fierce debates among economists. A principle people generally agree on is that efficiency is best served if the government develops techniques which are also used in the market system. This is the case with the European approach to controlling CO_2 emissions, which is based on negotiable emission standards, working as follows. Every year the European Commission sets the maximum permissible quantity of CO_2 which large energy users (electricity companies, the steel or chemical industries, etc.) are allowed to emit. Assume that the limit is one million tonnes. The European Commission then divides emissions rights totalling one million tonnes between the companies which emit CO_2. This distribution is free and generally in proportion to each company's past emissions. If the company wants to expand, it will need to emit more, and it can buy the right to do so on the market. These CO_2 emissions rights will typically be supplied by companies which emit less CO_2 than the rights they have been allocated. Supply and demand of emissions rights come together in a market and a price is established. The clever thing about this system is that the companies are incentivized to use production techniques which emit little CO_2, enabling them to sell their unused rights. This makes the quest for CO_2-efficient technologies profitable. We effectively simulate a market mechanism.

This system of imposing restrictions on the market is very attractive. It does, however, assume the existence of an institution outside the market, in this case the European Commission, to set the global emissions levels. The market cannot do this on its own strength.

In practice the European system of negotiable emissions rights shows how difficult it is for governments to impose such restrictions on the market. The intention was that the European Commission would reduce the quantity of global emissions rights, raising their price, which in turn would increasingly incentivize companies to use production techniques which involved low emissions. Unfortunately that has not worked so far. When the system started up in 2006, the price of a tonne of CO_2 was around 20 euros. Companies wanting to emit an extra tonne had to pay 20 euros, and companies managing to save a tonne of emissions were rewarded for their good behaviour with 20 euros. In 2014 the price of a tonne of CO_2 has collapsed to less than 5 euros. With the price so low, there is no longer much of an incentive to reduce emissions.

One of the main reasons for this failure is that the European Commission failed to stand up to intensive lobbying by the major energy-intensive industries, many of which received exemptions from their national governments. As a result the European Commission was far too generous in allocating CO_2 emissions rights. This over-supply is the main cause of the collapse of the price of CO_2.

So there are many problems with the practical implementation of government regulation. A method might sometimes seem desirable from a theoretical perspective, as in the case of CO_2 emissions rights, but not be chosen for practical reasons.

The Role of the Government: Public Goods

As we have discussed in detail, public goods do not arise automatically in a market system, mainly because the market system offers no solution to the free-rider behaviour of those who would like to benefit from public goods but do not want to pay for them. Again an external organization is needed to correct the market.

In democratic societies there is only one good way of achieving this. The scenario is as follows. Citizens indicate their preferences for public goods to the politicians who represent them. If a majority can be found in favour of building an extra railway line, for example, then politicians in a democratic country will listen and decide to do so, financing it through taxes. In actual fact, this is a very unattractive method because there is an element of compulsion involved. After all, there will be some opponents of the railway, who will also have to pay. Regrettably there is no alternative to this compulsion. As we saw previously, if funding is organized on a voluntary basis, there is a chance that the railway line will never be built, even if a large majority is in favour.

Here again the practical implementation of the theory is not straightforward. Often there is no consensus on the question of which and how many public goods are needed. Every decision to produce public goods also has side effects. The new railway, for example, will run on private land, which will have to be expropriated. The owners will not just give it up but will organize to disrupt the building of the railway (or prison, or waste incinerator, etc.).

We therefore need a strong government who can resist the pressure from interest groups. But how strong does the government need to be to do that? As strong as the Chinese government, which informs house owners a week before work starts on a new road that the bulldozers are on their way? We probably would not want that. We will return to this problem in the following chapters.

This theory on the method of tackling externalities and public goods is normative. It tells us what the government ought to do. It is important to know this, as it enables us to formulate the restrictions the government should set on the working of the market system, which should in principle prevent it from causing its own downfall.

The Role of the Government: Redistribution

In the previous chapter we saw that the market system is indifferent to income and wealth distribution. There may even be 'market equilibrium' when some people have no income and are dying of starvation. Many people, however, see such an equilibrium as unacceptable.

In order to keep the market system socially acceptable, and to avoid dissatisfaction turning into violent rejection, an institution outside the market is required to redistribute incomes. The market itself will not do this. Only the government is capable of it. Paradoxically enough it is the government which is able to rescue the market system by redistributing income and wealth. The owners of capital who have acquired a larger and larger piece of the economic pie over recent decades form a danger to the survival of capitalism. In this sense capitalists are the greatest enemies of capitalism.[16] In order to save the free market system, governments must tax the highest incomes and fortunes more heavily than they currently do.

Criticism of this approach rests on the idea that high taxes on top incomes have negative economic effects. People who earn millions and who are heavily taxed on their income above a million pounds, for example, would make less effort and show less initiative, which would negatively affect economic growth.

This vision is reflected in the form of a graph showing the relationship between equality and growth (see Figure 6.1). The horizontal axis shows the level of income equality, the vertical axis economic growth.

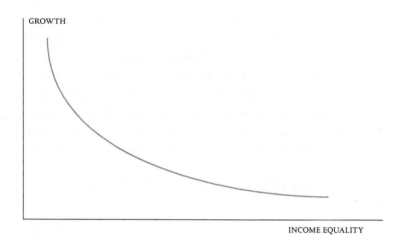

Figure 6.1. Trade-off between growth and income equality

The relationship is negative. The economists see this as a trade-off, where we must sacrifice one thing to gain another. If we want more growth, we must allow greater inequality. The prospect of earning a great deal of money encourages people to develop new initiatives, which eventually boosts economic growth.

There is a grain of truth to this theory. If everyone is equal then few people will be prepared to exert themselves to take initiatives, and economic growth will inevitably drop.

Of course the question is how great inequality can be permitted to become. Figure 6.1 shows that when equality tends towards zero (which implies maximum inequality), economic growth reaches its maximum. But that seems improbable. When inequality is at its highest—when one person (or family) takes all the income, leaving none for anyone else—then it is unlikely that growth will be high. On the contrary, in situations of such extreme inequality economic growth will collapse, if only because this will be a society of revolutions and political instability.

We can summarize it as follows. Too much equality (as in communist regimes) is not good for economic growth. Too much inequality is not good either, because it sets mechanisms in motion (such as social and political instability) which seriously endanger economic growth.

In a recent study the International Monetary Fund (IMF) explored the relationship between income inequality and economic growth in a large group of countries.[17] The results are surprising. The IMF comes to the conclusion that on average the countries which grow faster are those with less inequality. The IMF also finds that redistribution policies generally do not inhibit growth. These results cast doubt on the simple picture presented in Figure 6.1.

This also becomes clear from a comparison of Figures 6.2 and 6.3. Figure 6.2 gives the tax rates of the highest incomes from 1900 to 2010. (This is the same as Figure 1.3, with the addition of developments in rates since 1980.) Figure 6.3 represents economic growth in Western Europe and North America. We are now in a position to make a really

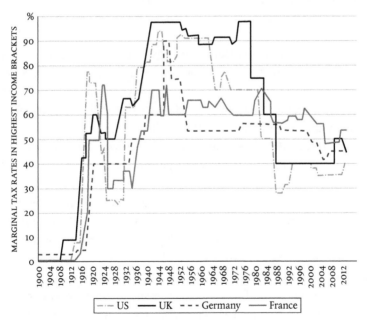

Figure 6.2. Highest personal income tax rates

Source: Piketty, <http://piketty.pse.ens.fr/en/capital21c2>

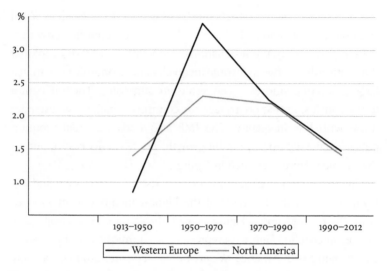

Figure 6.3. Average annual growth in per capita GDP (in %)
Source: Piketty, <http://piketty.pse.ens.fr/en/capital21c2>

remarkable observation. During the post-war period, when tax rates were at their highest, economic growth reached a historic high. Since the 1980s tax rates have been dramatically lowered under the influence of a new market philosophy, and from that point on economic growth also dropped sharply. The prediction that lowering tax rates on the highest incomes would encourage private initiative, in turn leading to more investments and higher economic growth, has not been supported at all.

The mechanisms which ensure that countries with greater income equality generally experience higher growth (as in Scandinavia) relate to the socially and politically stabilizing effects of greater equality.

The reason why a redistribution policy, focusing on taxing the very highest incomes, does not have a negative effect on economic growth can be explained as follows. Above a certain income, taxation barely affects effort. A top manager who earns ten million pounds does not work any harder than one who earns 'just' one million. At that level intrinsic motivation (pleasure in management and power) plays a much greater role. This means we can siphon off a much larger proportion of these top managers' financial remunerations without economic loss.

The case is similar to that of top footballers, who easily top ten million pounds per year in the Premier League. Would their game suffer if the government were to siphon off their earnings above the first million? In my view they would play just as well, perhaps even better, because people with such absurdly high incomes become arrogant and end up spending more and more time on activities other than sports.

A drastic redistribution policy aimed at the top earners with extremely high incomes would thus eventually benefit the market system, strengthening support in society for the system and preventing it from reaching its internal limits.

In Conclusion

This chapter has taught us what governments should do. We know what controls can rescue the free market from its downfall. These controls can only be implemented by governments. But is this knowledge sufficient? We often know perfectly well what governments should do. But that does not mean that governments will do what is necessary (as I suggested in this chapter). That is because governments are also subject to limitations. These make it difficult to impose what is good for society as a whole on individuals. Great discrepancies can exist between collective and individual rationality, in politics just as elsewhere. This is the subject of Chapter 7.

EXTERNAL LIMITS OF GOVERNMENTS

There are limits to governments which prevent politicians from following the normative prescriptions of economic theory. In this chapter we will address the external limits of governments. In Chapter 8 we will discuss their internal limits.

As in the market system, the external limits of governments relate to externalities. Here I will defend the following proposition. The fundamental task of governments is to promote the collective interest (for instance a clean environment) where the market does not. We saw above that the market fails in the face of externalities. When that happens governments must step in. However, as we saw previously, that is also the moment at which the discrepancy between individual and collective interests is widest. If there is no discrepancy, governments do not need to intervene. That is only necessary when the discrepancy is too large.

Government Action Struggles to Get off the Ground

This means that governments must step in in unfavourable circumstances. It is in cases of large differences between individual and collective interests that governments should take action. This makes government action extremely difficult.

If a company causes a great deal of pollution, this in fact indicates that from the perspective of society, production, employment, and profits are too high. In order to uphold the collective interest (in this case a clean environment), the government will need to impose a tax on the company, reducing production, employment, and profits. The more the company pollutes, the higher the tax will need to be and the greater the drop in production, employment, and profits.

There is no escaping it. In order to promote the collective interest, the government will have to harm private interests. What are the private interests in this case? We have the company shareholders, whose shares will drop in value; there are the managers, who will receive smaller bonuses; and there are the employees who will lose their jobs due to reduced production.

These private interests will organize to persuade politicians not to levy the environmental tax. The interests of the owners, managers, and employees clash with those of the many people harmed by pollution. The government will have to weigh up the interests of the two groups (which in fact overlap). That is not an easy task for various reasons.

Firstly, once again, there is an information problem. Given that it is very difficult to determine scientifically the magnitude of the harm from pollution, the information will almost inevitably be manipulated. The representatives of manufacturers in polluting industries will commission studies to downplay the impact of the pollution. For instance it recently transpired that large American companies subsidized reputable, 'independent' think tanks to carry out research to show that the negative effects of global warming were exaggerated.

Secondly there is also an important asymmetry in the collective action of different interest groups. This phenomenon has been brilliantly analysed by Mancur Olson in his book, *The Logic of Collective Action*.[18] The industries which pollute the environment have large, concentrated interests to defend. An environmental tax can have a substantial negative effect on the turnover and profit of polluting companies. They will therefore be prepared to commit considerable resources in order to combat an environmental tax. Since they are not so numerous, they will also find it easier to organize and take collective action. For the many millions of people bearing the costs of pollution the situation is different. They do not experience these costs in the same intense manner as the producers. The victims, although much more numerous, find it less easy to exert political influence, only succeeding if the costs of pollution are extremely high.

Democracy Helps

Governments must therefore mediate between the interests of the minority, which employs every means it can to ensure its interests are served, and a majority of people who incur damage. It is not clear beforehand which direction the government will take. Much will depend on the democratic quality of the institutions. In many countries the minority wins. In these countries the government systematically chooses in favour of the large polluting businesses. This is possible because there is no functioning democracy in place. Politicians are bribed by polluting companies, without any mechanism to put a stop to it. This is referred to as 'crony capitalism', where the government systematically defends capitalist interests. Companies exploit their labourers unpunished, destroy the environment, and conspire to push up prices. Politicians, who are bribed or even control large parts of the industry themselves, openly defend the capitalists. A symbiosis arises between government and capital.

In other countries the quality of the democratic authorities ensures that the voice of the majority dominates. This is the case, for example, in Scandinavian countries, where strong democratic institutions, including an independent press, counterbalance the polluting companies.

Daron Acemoglu and James Robinson distinguish here between inclusive and exclusive political systems.[19] An inclusive political system is based on the rule of law. It is an open system, in which all citizens can share in economic prosperity and have the chance to take initiatives. Exclusive political systems are closed systems, in which a small elite make the political and economic decisions and take a large proportion of the economic surplus for themselves. The majority of the population is excluded.

The problem of an exclusive political system is that the discrepancy between collective and individual interests is too great. The political pressure which the victims of pollution exert becomes ever greater. Since there are no democratic channels (such as elections), this political pressure must be exerted through protests, social action, and violence, destabilizing the system. This can lead to political upheaval which seriously damages the market system.

We run into the following paradox. Democracy is needed to safeguard capitalism in the long term. Democratic institutions make it possible to identify collective interests quickly and give them a voice. This forces politicians to promote collective interests instead of the individual interests of the rich and influential. In this way democratic institutions bring stability. The discrepancy between collective and individual interests does not grow to excessive proportions.

In his impressive book Martin Gilens[20] analyses how the American political system promotes the interests of those with the highest incomes. This is closely related to the fact that in the US money is the determining factor in winning elections. To a certain extent it could be said that the US is also a victim of crony capitalism. That makes it very difficult for the government to take care of the public domain, such as the environment.

Better known examples of crony capitalism appear in countries in Asia, Africa, and Latin America. Many countries are also unstable. In time there will be revolution and violence, which will damage the mechanism of the free market system. As I concluded previously when I talked about inequality, the true enemies of capitalism are the capitalists themselves.

External Limits of Governments

I argued above that political action to reduce the discrepancy between individual and collective interests is difficult to get off the ground, but let us now assume that the government is working to promote the collective interest, even when that is at the expense of private interests. Where do the limits of necessary government action come from?

I argued earlier that every government action which attempts to defend collective interests will harm private interests. Such policies are also coercive in character. To start with, taxes must be levied, and they are imposed on individuals against their will. Furthermore, the entirety of the collective action is aimed at changing the behaviour of individuals. That can be achieved gently through the price mechanism. For example a tax on products which pollute the environment will raise their price. Consumers remain free to buy the product, but because it has become more expensive, many consumers will buy less of it. Coercion is unavoidable, even with this soft approach, because it involves levying a tax. There are some harmful activities, however, which cannot be tackled softly and must be prohibited. Punishments follow for those who fail to respect the prohibition.

These are top-down control mechanisms which attempt to rein in individuals, distancing us from the market system, which is based on free enterprise. In the market system no one orders the baker to bake bread. He does so of his own free will and in pursuit of profit. He decides for himself how long to work and how much bread to bake.

The problem of lack of freedom crops up particularly in the case of the environment. Deterioration of the environment in many countries, and especially global warming, creates existential problems for the human race. There is rising pressure on governments to do something about it, leading to more top-down control, which often feels stifling. People feel they are losing their freedom and respond by rejecting the policies involved. In many countries, especially the US, this takes the form of negationism, where people deny that there is a problem. As I argued above, part of this strategy of denial is inspired by self-interest and pursuit of profits among industrial companies. But it is also in part a psychological response to an ever more controlling and even repressive environmental policy. This limits what governments can do when they prioritize collective interests.

In Conclusion

We observe that the fundamental cause of limits to government action is the same discrepancy between individual and collective rationality which limits the market system. Individuals resist the attempts of government to harm private interests in favour of the collective. The discrepancy here works in a different direction from the market system, where individuals make decisions which harm the collective good. Here the opposite applies. The government which steps in to defend the collective interest comes up against individual interests, restricting their radius of action.

The big challenge of governments is therefore to bridge the difference between individual and collective rationality. This is best achieved in democratic forms of government of an inclusive type. Inclusivity makes it easier for the government to achieve consensus on decisions necessary to promote collective interests, as in such systems the costs and benefits of government interventions can be more easily spread over the entire population. The individuals who are harmed by the collective action are compensated by the others, so they will agree more easily to interventions. This may mean that the decision process in such inclusive democratic societies can take a long time, but when decisions are made they are backed by broader support.

Exclusive authoritarian regimes have serious problems gaining support because it is easier for private interests to infiltrate such political systems. The result is that the discrepancy between private and collective interests is greater than in democratic societies.

CHAPTER 8

INTERNAL LIMITS OF GOVERNMENTS

W e have seen that the free market mainly appeals to individuals' rational, calculating capacities (System II) at the expense of their emotions. This leaves many people dissatisfied about the cold, inhuman character of the market system, leading to its rejection.

Governments as Magnets for System I

This dissatisfaction creates an opportunity for governments to fill the emotional gap left by the free market and to focus on System I, which steers our emotions. Many emotions therefore find an outlet through government. Some of these emotions are positive, such as the sense of fairness, which is difficult to express in the market because it plays no role there. The urge for fair distribution will therefore seek an outlet in government. Politicians translate this drive into income redistribution policies.

Some feelings, however, are negative. For example, many people harbour a fear of the unknown, especially when it comes to foreign countries. Immigration is seen by many as a great danger. The market has no feelings on the matter and is indifferent to whether the consumer is a native of the country or an immigrant. Companies are in fact more likely to support immigration, because it gives them access to cheaper labour. For this reason people who fear immigration will appeal to governments to restrict it.

Governments are therefore the mechanism by which our emotions (System I) are expressed. Market and government become specialized in different areas, the market appealing to System II while governments call on System I. It may be useful to investigate the reasons for this specialization in more detail.

The market specializes in appealing to System II for a simple reason. The consumer has a limited budget and must make decisions. This compels him to use System II, the calculating part of his brain. The wrong choice by the consumer is immediately punished, so he has strong incentives to deal rationally with the limited budget he has to spend.

When making political choices, on the other hand (to vote for left-wing or right-wing governments, for example), people face no budget restrictions. The voter is not immediately financially affected by the choice he makes. This also relates to the fact that the influence of the individual voter on the final result of the election is infinitely small. As a result, the voter will be led more by his emotional side when he votes for one or other party. How do the politicians look? How trustworthy do they seem? The answers to such questions carry considerable weight in the polling booth.

This opens up the opportunity for politically minded entrepreneurs to appeal to System I. Often they will magnify emotions, as we have recently seen. On 1 January 2014 the borders were opened for free immigration from Bulgaria and Romania within the EU. Politicians in many EU countries jumped at the opportunity to express their concern about the dangers of immigration from these countries. The fear already present among many citizens was magnified by this. It eventually proved unjustified, as immigration from these countries remained limited, but even that fact has not really reduced fears. In many countries, including the UK, politicians continue to fan the flames.

The market's specialization in System II and government specialization in System I result in a focus on efficiency problems in markets, while governments focus on distribution problems. We discuss this theme further in the following section.

Governments Focus mainly on Distribution Problems

People have a very strong sense of fairness. This has nothing to do with jealousy. It is simply hard-wired into each of us. Generally we have no problem with people who perform well earning a great deal. Performance can be rewarded. What we find morally reprehensible is people being rewarded when they do not deserve it. Our moral sensibilities are offended when we discover that people have become rich through theft, betrayal, or corruption.

The sense of fairness seems to be universal. This has been confirmed in many experiments involving the ultimatum game, which works as follows. John receives one hundred pounds. He has to share this sum with Peter. John can choose to give Peter any sum between one and one hundred. But Peter is allowed to refuse John's gift. In that case both end up with nothing. The question is how much John will give Peter. If John's rational System II has the upper hand, he will give Peter one pound. Rationality as economists define it implies that both players will choose to receive more rather than less. John makes the most of his position, keeping ninety-nine pounds, and Peter is happy too, because one pound is better than none. He will not refuse John's gift, as that would mean that he would receive nothing. System II is thus satisfied.

When this experiment is carried out, however, the prediction based on rational behaviour is not borne out at all. The experiment has been repeated hundreds of times in different countries and cultures. A gift of one pound (or any other currency) is unanimously rejected because people think it is unfair. They prefer to receive zero pounds rather than a sum they perceive to be unjust. They choose nothing in preference to one pound because this is the only way they can punish the other player, satisfying their sense of fairness.

The many experiments with the ultimatum game suggest that the acceptable distribution is around 70/30. There is some variation, but the results indicate that a sense of fairness wins out over pure profit motive. System I dominates System II.

So people like to punish unfairness, even if they pay a financial price for it. Our sense of fairness is deep-rooted. It is often affronted by the free market, which is indifferent to the question of whether the distribution of income is fair. People, however, are not indifferent. They therefore turn to governments when they consider a particular distribution unfair. As we saw previously, the distribution of income in the market can be very unequal. That is the breeding ground for governments. The result is that much of the job of politicians relates to redistribution.

This tendency is also illustrated in Figure 8.1, which shows the magnitude of spending on social security in a number of OECD countries since 1985. We notice a number of interesting phenomena. In 2009 spending on social security in most countries was more than fifty per cent of all government spending. That is to say, more than

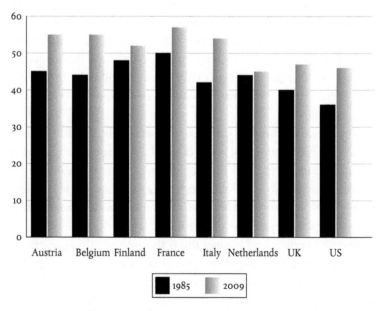

Figure 8.1. Spending on social security as % of government spending
Source: OECD, *Social Expenditure*, <http://stats.oecd.org/Index.aspx?QueryId=4549>

half what governments did in those countries related to redistribution. We also note that since 1985 the share of social security spending in the same countries has risen sharply, showing that redistribution is becoming increasingly important.

Winner Takes All

In sport the competitor in first place takes the top prize. The difference between those in first and second place is often negligible, but the winner generally receives many times the reward of the competitor placed second. The winner-takes-all phenomenon so important in sport can also be found in economics.

Take the market of top managers. The selection mechanism which leads to the selection of a top manager is a competition, with the winner receiving the big prize. The second in line receives nothing, or only a fraction of what the winner comes away with. Generally the winner is only marginally better than those in second and third place, but his reward is many times that of the runners-up.

In these markets a big discrepancy arises between reward and performance. The reward for the winner (top manager) is many times that of the second and third-placed candidate for the job, although the winner is not notably better than the runners-up. Generally top managers will convince themselves that they really are better than the others, but that is based on inflated egos.

In the last thirty years the salaries of top managers have risen enormously. While the average CEO of a large American company in 1975 earned thirty times that of the average employee at his company, in 2008 that had risen to 300 times as much. Has the American CEO become so much more productive or creative in the last thirty years? That is not particularly likely. A more plausible explanation is that the winner-takes-all structure has become ever more important. This is probably also the underlying cause of the spectacular rise in income of the top one per cent in the US income distribution.

Although these tendencies are less striking in Europe than in the US, we see a substantial rise in the remuneration of European top management in comparison with that of ordinary staff. In the United Kingdom the CEO's salary has risen from forty-six times to 120 times that of the average employee in the last decade. It is unlikely that top managers in Europe have improved so much in recent decades. Here too the law of winner takes all plays an ever greater role.

This creates a great tension between Systems I and II in many people. If the market system leads to such salaries, which barely show any relationship to performance, emotions gain the upper hand and governments come under pressure to call a halt to the market, imposing rules or taxes to correct the inequality. French president François Hollande used this to impose a tax of seventy-five percent on incomes above one million euros. Nowadays such a move is received with disbelief or even derision, especially by the Anglo-Saxon press, but this is something that can change. If inequality continues to grow, it creates a political breeding ground for moves in the direction of tax increases in other countries. We should not forget history either. As mentioned above, tax rates for the highest incomes rose spectacularly after the shock of the Great Depression. What seems ridiculous today will look different if the increase in inequality is not stopped.

Governments specialize in distribution problems, but they have their limits. We explore two here. The first relates to efficiency, the second to the internal balance between Systems I and II.

First Limit: Redistribution at the Expense of Efficiency

Many economists take it for granted that there will be economic loss when governments redistribute too much, as the economy becomes less efficient. That was clear under the communist regimes dominant in large areas of the world in the previous century. In these regimes there was a belief that incomes should not be distributed based on the market system, founded mainly on performance. Everyone should be equal, was the motto under communism. This kind of system of course leads to a great loss of efficiency. Who would be willing to exert themselves and perform well if effort and achievement were not rewarded? The result was that the economies in these countries ground to a halt.

So the economists are right that too much redistribution in time leads to great economic losses. In Chapter 6 we discussed the trade-off between economic growth and equality. If we want greater equality, we pay a price for it in the form of reduced economic growth. In essence this is also the question discussed here. Too much redistribution in time leads to a loss of economic efficiency and a concomitant drop in prosperity.

Figure 8.2 shows the relationships between equality and efficiency. The horizontal axis indicates equality, with greater equality of income distribution the further we go to the right. The vertical axis gives a measure of efficiency. The higher we move on this axis the better the economy runs and the higher the level of material prosperity. The trade-off is presented by the negatively sloped curve: as we strive for income equality, we lose efficiency and prosperity.

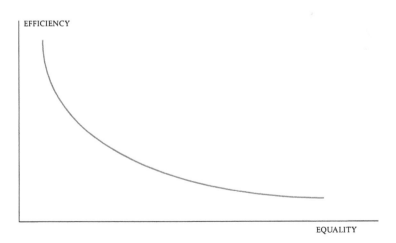

Figure 8.2. Trade-off between efficiency and equality

The trade-off between efficiency and equality is an important limit to a redistribution policy. The loss of prosperity can be so great that many people reject the system. This reaction was an important factor in the implosion of communist regimes, which were no longer capable of guaranteeing minimal material prosperity. They had clearly exceeded their limits and were punished. With the exception of North Korea, communist regimes have disappeared from the world as political systems.

We therefore conclude that neither excessive equality nor excessive inequality is good for economic efficiency. The relationship between equality and efficiency is different from that of Figure 8.2, though. A better representation appears in Figure 8.3. When equality is very low (extreme inequality), we also see very low economic efficiency, probably because extreme inequality is accompanied by a great deal of internal conflict, which disrupts society. In an unstable political and social environment the market system cannot function properly and

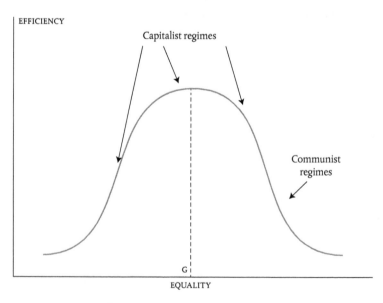

Figure 8.3. Relationship between efficiency and equality

economic efficiency is low. Greater equality will lead to greater stability, increasing efficiency. Too much equality ultimately will reduce efficiency.

Where should we place different countries in this graph? The position of the communist regimes of the last century is clearly to the right of point G. The economic equality of most people (not the elite, of course) resulted in a complete lack of initiative and creativity and a great loss of material well-being (efficiency).

Where do we place the other countries which have almost all adopted some form or other of capitalism? That is much more difficult. Some can probably also be found to the right of point G, but it is likely that many are on the left. There are Latin American countries where great inequality has in fact crippled growth in material prosperity. We also see inequality increasing in many Western countries from 1980, which coincides with the period in which economic growth has slowed.

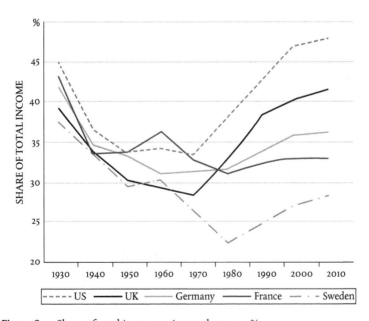

Figure 8.4. Share of total income going to the top 10%

Figure 8.4 again shows the development of income inequality expressed as the share of total income going to the top ten per cent (see also Figure 4.2). Figure 8.5 is the same as Figure 6.3 from Chapter 6, showing the development of economic growth. Here again we observe something remarkable: during the period from 1950 to 1970 inequality in income in the US and the important Western European countries hit a historic low. This was also the period in which economic growth reached a historic high. From 1980 income inequality has risen spectacularly in most countries (with the exception of France) and from that moment on economic growth has dropped significantly.

From the discussion above we can tell that there is a good chance that many capitalist countries are to the left of point G in Figure 8.3. For those countries the rule is that more equality could promote material prosperity, as confirmed by the IMF study we discussed in Chapter 6, showing that greater equality in industrial countries does not lead to lower economic growth. In fact the reverse seems to be true.

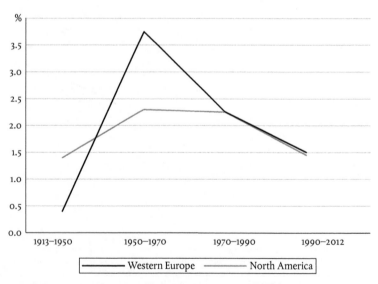

Figure 8.5. Average annual growth in per capita GDP (in %)

Source: Piketty, <http://piketty.pse.ens.fr/en/capital21c2>

Our conclusion holds up. Governments can only go so far in redistribution before material prosperity is damaged. In Western Europe and America we are still far from that point, but if it happens, governments will reach their limits and there is a good chance that their role in the economy will be scaled back.

Second Limit: Balance between Systems I and II

Governments appeal to System I and therefore focus mainly on redistribution problems, but this clashes with the need to develop System II as well. System II allows individuals to determine what is good or bad for themselves. Governments are nannying, nagging organizations, imposing rules and regulations. The more governments work on redistribution, the more they have to tax people and the more they have to limit individual freedom.

When governments decide to redistribute they do not ask who wants to participate. Everyone is obliged to do so, even those who have voted against it, for instance because they have a high income. They cannot opt out of the policy, unless they move to another country. There is something unattractive about a system of this kind involving compulsion. Few individuals like the idea. Compulsion must therefore be exercised in moderation; otherwise people revolt against it.

Limits to Social Security

Social security was developed in response to the blind nature of the market system. As I stressed before, the free market is indifferent to inequality and poverty. If people are affected by a calamity and are unable to perform, leaving them excluded, this does not disturb the market equilibrium. The market system continues, as if nothing has happened. That clashes with our sense of fairness. This is the fundamental reason why social security exists.

But social security systems can in turn come up against their limits. Social security, like any insurance mechanism, leads to moral hazard, by which economists mean the following. Whenever we insure ourselves against a particular risk, our vigilance with respect to that risk will be reduced. If we take out insurance against theft, we might neglect to instal the latest security technology in our homes. We are insured, after all.

The same can happen with social security. Insurance against unemployment can lead the unemployed to search less intensely for jobs. This response will be stronger the closer the unemployment benefits are to net salaries. That is currently an issue for many unskilled workers in most Western European countries. Many unskilled jobs are not particularly interesting. No wonder the unskilled and unemployed have little incentive to look for another job or to move house if remuneration for a new job is barely above unemployment benefits. The unemployed thus end up entangled in a trap from which they cannot easily extricate themselves.

When such understandable and rational behaviour becomes too widespread, the social security system comes up against its limits. This behaviour, although rational, conflicts with our sense of fairness. This is paradoxical to a certain extent. On the one hand social security exists because inequality and poverty offend our sense of fairness. At the same time a sense of fairness is what sets limits on excesses in social security. This involves a different aspect of our sense of fairness. We consider it fair that people are rewarded for effort and achievement, and are angry when we discover that people have been rewarded when they have not performed well enough. That applies to the banker who receives a bonus for a substandard performance, just as it does to the unemployed person who enjoys social benefits without making an effort to find a job.

In recent decades social security in many European countries has run into this problem of moral hazard. The perception that many people benefit from the system at the expense of those who work undermines support from society for social security. This allows politicians to paint themselves as the ones who will combat 'social welfare fraud'.

It is clear that the problem of moral hazard must be tackled. If it is not, then the system will be rejected by society. Some countries, particularly the Scandinavian countries, have succeeded relatively well in keeping moral hazard under control. They achieve this through a policy of activation of the unemployed, encouraging and helping them to re-enter the job market. The effect of the policy is that despite the generous Scandinavian social security system, employees keep working for a long time and the unemployed are not unemployed for long.

In continental European countries (Belgium, France, Italy) the situation is rather different. In these countries the social security system has failed to solve the problem of moral hazard. The system provides too many financial incentives not to work, undermining itself in two ways: firstly financially, because if too few people work, social security payments have to be cut constantly, eroding the system; and secondly socially, as the perception that too many people are free-riders undermines society's support. Without support the system cannot stay afloat.

Over recent decades there has been a great deal of research into the performance of different models of social security. The literature normally makes a distinction between four models: Scandinavian, continental European, Mediterranean, and Anglo-Saxon. Here we will not go into the details of the classifications (see Boeri 2002 and Sapir 2005).[21] There is a broad consensus that the model which works the best is the Scandinavian model, where performance translates to a low level of poverty, low unemployment, and high employment. The other models exhibit a much poorer performance in these areas.

The problem with social security is interesting to the extent that both its existence and its limits relate to a sense of fairness shared by most individuals. It is therefore important to find a balance which satisfies this emotional motivation. Otherwise we will move from one extreme to another.

Currently the social security system in many countries is being dismantled. This is very much the case in eurozone countries which have had to introduce radical programmes of spending cuts as a result of the sovereign debt crisis. In many of these countries (Greece, Spain,

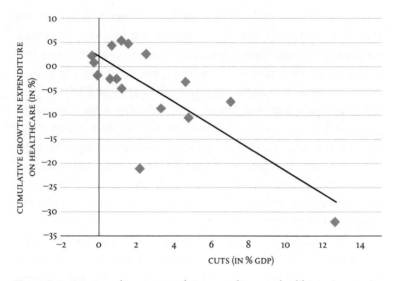

Figure 8.6. Cuts in real-terms growth in expenditure on healthcare (2009–11)

Source: Eurostat

Portugal, Ireland) social security has been hit extremely hard. We can see this in Figure 8.6. The horizontal axis shows the magnitude of budget cuts from 2009 to 2011. The vertical axis shows the drop in expenditure for healthcare in the same countries. Each point represents a country. We can see that countries which have cut the most (in percentage of GDP) are also the ones which have reduced spending on healthcare the most.

If we go too far in dismantling social security, we give the market system free rein, resulting in inequality and poverty. This continues until people react against the market system again.

In Conclusion

Governments are called on because the market system appeals too little to the emotional System I. Governments must correct the great inequalities a market system can cause, but they can go too far in this, running up against their own internal limits, which relate to the fact that System II becomes repressed. This is the system which causes us to long for rational, autonomous choices. When this repression becomes too great, there is a great loss of economic efficiency. If this loss is too great, society rejects the system, as happened with the communist regimes of the twentieth century.

The internal limits of government action, however, can also spring from System I. We have seen that our sense of fairness causes us to long for a system of social security, which can only be guaranteed by the government. But if the government does not keep moral hazard under control, a backlash occurs, also springing from a sense of fairness offended by too many 'free-riders'. That feeling can become so strong that social security is cut back.

CHAPTER 9

WHO IS IN CHARGE?
MARKET OR GOVERNMENT?

Discussions on the role of the market and government have been raging for centuries, generally between people who believed either that the market system was the foundation of economic organization or that that task was reserved for government. In the view of the former group the market took priority over government, and vice versa for the latter. Both thus argued for a hierarchy between market and government.

We can envisage that idea of hierarchy in the shape of a pyramid. According to the market fundamentalists it looks like Figure 9.1. The market system forms the foundation where economic value is created. That economic value makes it possible to maintain the public sector. Without the market there is no government. According to this vision the public sector is in a sense parasitic. It sucks resources out of the market sector. If that happens too much, the market sector is in danger.

That vision is very popular among businessmen and employer organizations, who like to see themselves as the hard workers sustaining a superstructure (the public sector). They also tend to think of the market sector as productive and the public sector as unproductive, profiting from the productivity of the market. A similar image exists of the hierarchy between industry and services. We will discuss this separately at the end of this chapter.

For government fundamentalists there is also a hierarchy, but it is precisely the reverse, giving us the pyramid shown in Figure 9.2. This

Figure 9.1. Market/government hierarchy according to market fundamentalists

Figure 9.2. Market/government hierarchy according to government fundamentalists

group believes it is the government which forms the foundation for the functioning of the market. The government makes it possible to establish and enforce property rights. Without those property rights no market system can work and the law of the jungle prevails. More generally, without the rule of law, which can only be guaranteed by government, a stable market system based on contractual relationships is impossible.

Without government there is also no infrastructure, and without infrastructure no transport or specialization is possible. Think of countries such as the Congo, where the infrastructure has disappeared and the economy cannot get off the ground. The government also enables the organization of universal primary education. Without literacy and numeracy, industrial activity is impossible. According to this vision the public sector is no less productive than the market sector. In fact, the productivity of the market sector is derived from that of the public sector, which ensures the existence of public goods essential to the existence of the market.

This hierarchical thinking is wrong. Both visions only tell part of the story. It is true that without government no market system is possible. However, it is equally true that the expansion of the public sector, as we have seen in Western countries, is only possible with a productive market sector. Both sides need each other. There is no hierarchy between the two. Neither one is more important than the other. We might envisage the situation with Figure 9.3.

The old discussion as to whether the market is more important than government or vice versa is pointless. The only question worth asking is how the division of labour between market and government can best be organized. This division of labour must start out from the ideas we developed in the previous chapters, where we saw that both market and government have their limits.

If the government does not succeed in making those who generate external costs from market activities pay for them, then at some point the market system will come to an end. In the same way we can conclude that a government which does not succeed in providing essential public goods such as infrastructure, law and order, public safety, and education will lead the way to the downfall of the market system.

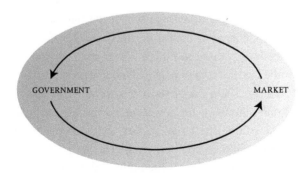

Figure 9.3. Non-hierarchical relationship between government and market

While the market needs a government to survive, the government also needs the market. Governments can only really ensure collective goods and services in the presence of a strong free market. The communist 'experiments' of the last century have shown us this. These experiments assumed that the government had to make all economic decisions, without appealing to market mechanisms. There were spectacular inefficiencies in communist countries, which led to people being deprived of many elementary goods and services. The system led to permanent scarcity. Furthermore, due to the weight of the public sector, technological development came to a standstill, and with it material well-being.

On Productivity, Labour Costs, and the Public Sector

The vision of the public sector as leeching off the market sector, and thereby constituting a severe burden, also colours the entire discussion of labour costs. In Northern Europe labour costs are very high, as is clear from Figure 9.4. We observe the highest hourly wages in Europe (in 2013) in the countries of Northern Europe, especially Scandinavia. This figure also shows that the EU countries which have encountered serious financial problems have much lower hourly wages than the top five in the list. This suggests that high labour costs need not necessarily lead to problems. They can also be an advantage.

However, that is not the way in which the high labour costs in many Northern European countries are generally interpreted. The traditional analysis is that those high labour costs are the result of a high tax burden in the form of personal income tax and contributions to social security. These social security contributions and taxes are seen as a burden imposed on businesses to finance the government and the public sector. These two sectors 'leech off' productive businesses, undermining their competiveness. The burden must therefore be reduced in order to guarantee the future viability of the firms. This analysis conceals the same implicit idea of hierarchy.

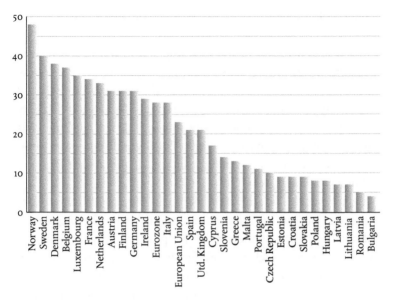

Figure 9.4. Gross hourly labour costs in 2013 (euros)

Source: Eurostat

These high labour costs, however, can also be interpreted another way, namely as a result of high productivity. In that case high labour costs are a sign of prosperity, not a burden.

The high labour costs in Northern Europe are the result of a more fundamental and essentially positive phenomenon known as productivity growth. Technological progress enables workers to be increasingly productive. Nowadays the same amount is produced by less than half the number of workers it would have taken thirty years ago. This growth in productivity is specific to industry and is much less prevalent in the service sector.

Productivity growth leads to an important phenomenon, namely high wages. That is good news. High wages in Northern Europe reflect a long industrial and economic development which has raised productivity to an unprecedented level, allowing workers to benefit as they should. A high wage is first and foremost a reward for skill, knowledge, and effort. It is the expression of the high level of prosperity we have achieved.

This brings us to the following insight. Growth in productivity, which is unstoppable in industry, inevitably leads to job losses. Those who keep their jobs enjoy this productivity growth through high wages. High salaries are not the cause of the job losses in industry; rather both result from productivity growth. This will continue, causing more job losses and high wages. Employers like to keep labour costs down. Well, they will only succeed if they manage to halt technological progress.

High wages as a reflection of high productivity add value to society, which can put the economy in a virtuous circle. This happens as follows. High wages supported by high productivity make it possible to provide services such as education, healthcare, social facilities, the service sector, travel, law and order, public safety, and so on. That not only creates many jobs, but also increases general well-being and the level of knowledge of employees.

All these effects in turn boost productivity levels, thus benefiting companies and industry. Nowhere is this virtuous circle as conspicuous as in the Scandinavian countries. The high salaries in these countries are also a lever, increasing the well-being and knowledge of employees. As a result the Scandinavian countries, despite high salaries, belong to the most competitive countries in the world.

This is apparent from the competitiveness ranking assigned to them by the World Economic Forum, which is based on a multidimensional analysis of the concept of competitiveness. Beyond narrow price competitiveness, this encompasses all other factors which influence a country's competitiveness, such as the quality of public administration, education, science and technology, law and order, public safety, stability, and so on. According to this index, Finland and Sweden, for example, have been ranked third and sixth respectively in the list of the most competitive countries.

In fact it turns out that there is a positive relationship between salary levels and a country's competitiveness. That relationship is

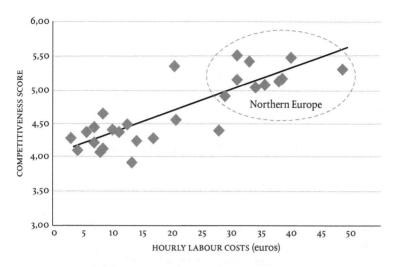

Figure 9.5. Hourly labour costs and national competitiveness

Source: Eurostat (hourly labour costs) and World Economic Forum <http://www.weforum.org/issues/global-competitiveness>

shown in Figure 9.5. The horizontal axis shows hourly labour costs. They are the same labour costs as in Figure 9.4. The competitiveness score (as calculated by the World Economic Forum) is on the vertical axis. The higher the score, the higher the competitiveness. The data are remarkable. It appears that on average countries with high labour costs are also highly competitive. Without exception these are Northern European countries. High salaries are therefore no obstacle to high competitiveness; in fact, they promote competitiveness.

High Labour Costs and Prosperity

The high labour costs in the north and west of Europe are the definitive sign of a high level of prosperity. In this sense we should cherish those high labour costs, instead of attacking them as employer organizations have done for decades. Instead of complaining about high labour costs it would be better to embrace the challenge and develop new goods and services.

High labour costs resulting from high productivity have made something else possible. They have also generated the means for expanding collective facilities and social security. As we have argued, these are needed to correct the problematic features of the market system. Without these corrections the market system heads towards its limits and will be rejected at some point.

The Illusion of Shifting the Burden

The high burden employers have to pay in labour costs is a thorn in their side. Countless proposals have been formulated to reduce these burdens. The most popular idea is a shift of the employer's contribution to a tax on consumption (VAT). The proponents of this approach hope to reduce labour costs substantially this way. Higher consumption tax might cause prices to rise, but that is compensated by lower labour costs enabling employers to lower their prices. It is therefore seen as a win-win situation: employers enjoy lower labour costs, while employees maintain the same net wages. Since consumption prices do not rise, employees' purchasing power also remains unchanged.

So could it be that a free lunch exists after all? Alas, it remains a myth. Such a shift will only have a limited effect on labour costs. Why?

A crucial point in the logic of those advocating a shift of the burden is that the employers will lower production prices so that the higher VAT does not lead to a rise in price for the consumer. However, that is rather unlikely. The most important reason why consumer prices will rise as a result of raising VAT relates to imports. Foreign producers do not enjoy the reduction in the burden on employers, but they are confronted with a rise in VAT when selling domestically. They will pass on the rise (in part or in full) to domestic consumers.

Besides this direct effect of the VAT rise on consumer prices, there is also an indirect effect. The domestic producers, who are confronted with price rises from their foreign competitors, will seize the opportunity offered by the shift of labour costs to VAT to expand their profit margins. That is easy because the competitors have raised their prices to consumers. Domestic producers will do the same to a greater or lesser extent.

The rise in VAT will therefore inevitably lead to a rise in consumer prices, reducing purchasing power among employees and raising demands on wages in order to maintain their purchasing power. This mechanism eventually limits the effect on labour costs of shifting the burden from employers to consumption tax.

Advocates of this shift see it as a win–win situation because they are only considering a partial analysis. Economists aim to produce an analysis taking into account all the effects. They call this a general equilibrium analysis.

How important is the general equilibrium effect? This is, in the end, an empirical question. We can look at the facts to find the answer. Figure 9.6 shows labour costs (on the vertical axis) and employer contributions as a percentage of labour costs (on the horizontal

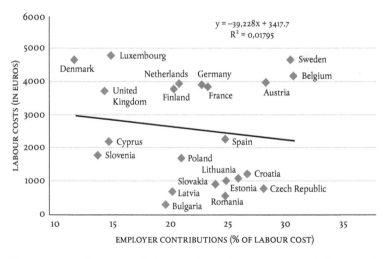

Figure 9.6. Employer contributions and monthly labour costs (industry and services, excluding public services) in EU (2007)

Source: Eurostat

axis) in EU countries in 2007. The most remarkable point is the fact that the level of the employers' social security contributions has no influence on labour costs. The regression line is even slightly negative, but the negative trend is not significant. The correct conclusion based on Figure 9.6 is that there is no significant relationship between the level of employer contributions and labour costs in EU countries.

This directly refutes what proponents of shifting the burden tell us. The countries with the lowest social security contributions do not have lower labour costs as a result. This is because in these countries social security is financed by taxes on consumption and income. The shift from employers' contributions to a different form of taxation is not paired with lower labour costs because, as we have argued, employees experiencing higher taxes on consumption and income will attempt to compensate for these by demanding higher wages.

It may be interesting to zoom in on the Northern European countries in the sample. These are the countries with the highest labour costs. We separate these countries out in Figure 9.7. In these countries

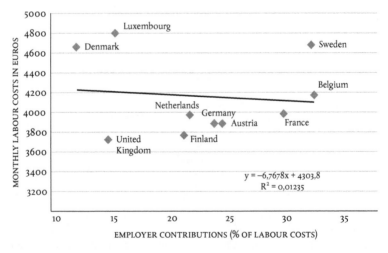

Figure 9.7. Employer contributions and monthly labour costs (2007)

Source: Eurostat

too there is no significant relationship between the level of employer contributions and labour costs. Countries imposing light burdens on employers (Denmark and Luxembourg) have labour costs no lower than countries with high employer burdens (Belgium and Sweden).

The contrast between Belgium and Denmark is interesting in this respect. Belgium has the highest employers' contributions in the EU and Denmark the lowest. Are labour costs lower in Denmark than in Belgium? No, in fact the opposite is the case. This relates to the fact that consumption prices for a number of much-used goods (such as cars) are much higher in Denmark than in Belgium. Danish workers also want cars, and for that they need a higher net salary.

It is an illusion to think that shifting the burden will magically reduce labour costs by a significant amount. Labour costs only fall if total government spending, and spending on social security in particular, drops. After all, it is the level of spending which determines pressure from taxes. Inevitably, the lion's share of the taxes will have to come out of labour. But a reduction in global government spending, including spending on social security, is precisely what most people want to avoid, and with good reason. The collective services are an essential element in the equilibrium between market and government. Without these services the market system is condemned to failure.

Can we not solve the problem of financing social security through a wealth tax? Instead of taxing workers, surely we should make the owners of capital pay for social security? I address this important question in Chapter 12. There I argue that a wealth tax is absolutely essential. The way in which such a tax has to be structured, however, results in the total revenues for government being relatively limited. As a consequence the wealth tax can only make a limited contribution to financing social security.

It is also important that government delivers the collective services efficiently. If these services are inefficient, the burdens on the private sector will be too heavy. The emphasis should therefore be on developing mechanisms to make government services more targeted, rather than on a hocus-pocus burden-shifting operation.

In Conclusion

In this chapter we have seen that the high labour costs in Northern Europe are a sign of a high level of prosperity. These high labour costs are the result of high productivity, which generates purchasing power, allowing people to buy new goods and services. More importantly, the high level of income which comes with higher productivity also generates the means to expand collective services and social security. These services form a necessary counterweight against a market system which is seen as cold and unfair. Without these corrections the market system approaches its limits and will be rejected at some point.

High salaries are also a symbol of the fact that our economic system has evolved into a mixture of market and state. Without government to provide public goods and social security, a market system cannot survive. At the same time a strong market system generates the resources for a strong social security system. Market and state are like twin brothers, inseparable and serving to reinforce one another. That is also apparent from the data on competitiveness and labour costs. The Scandinavian countries, which have the highest labour costs, belong to the most competitive countries in the world.

We also saw that there is a school of thought, mainly popular among businessmen which states that labour costs can be substantially supressed by reducing employer contributions to social security and compensating for these by raising other taxes, mainly on consumption (particularly VAT). We have observed, however, that the level of employer contributions has no influence on the level of labour costs. A reduction in labour costs is not a technical operation without associated costs. Such a reduction can only be achieved through a drastic cut in government spending on the public sector.

Attacks on high labour costs are therefore attacks on the corrections the government has applied to the market system over the years.

Box 9.1. A Hierarchy of Economic Values?

It is a popular idea in the business world that economics involves a hierarchy of values. To put it differently, not all economic activities are equally valuable. The economy might be seen as forming a pyramid. The foundation consists of the manufacturing sector (which more or less coincides with industry). This is the sector which makes prosperity possible and supports the other economic activities. Above this foundation you then find sectors such as transport, financial services, marketing, and accounting. These create less value and so are less essential. Right at the top of the pyramid are local services, healthcare, and of course the public sector. These are the least valuable sectors. Without the creation of economic value by industry, this superstructure cannot exist. (See Figure 9.8.)

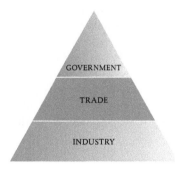

Figure 9.8. Hierarchy of economic activity: business view

   This popular idea is very old indeed. It originated from an eighteenth century French school of economic thought, the Physiocrats, who believed that agriculture formed the base of the economic pyramid and that the other sectors could only exist by its grace. Later Marx adopted this idea, but placed material production (industry) at the base.
   Economists have abandoned this idea of a hierarchy of economic activities, and with good reason. Today's economists start out from the idea that the economic value of goods and services is determined

(Cont.)

Box 9.1. Continued

by people's willingness to pay. It is meaningless to state that the economic value of a good is greater because it is made by industry; or that an evening out at a restaurant is less economically valuable than a material product from the manufacturing sector.

But without the manufacturing industry, the Physiocrats and Marxists will argue, the service sector cannot exist. That is true. But let us apply the same criterion to industry. Imagine what would happen if the education sector did not exist. People would not be able to read, write, or calculate. Would industry exist then? Of course not. We would be living in the Stone Age. We could just as easily build a different economic pyramid, with education at the base to ensure that people acquire the knowledge to be able to work in industry.

As argued in this chapter, we can draw other pyramids, for instance with the public sector at the base, to ensure law and order and public safety, without which there would be no property rights and no industry.

The moral of the story is that there is no hierarchy of economic values. Industry needs the service sector (education, law and order, public safety, etc.). Without these services industry cannot exist and no economic value can be created. The opposite is equally true. Without the value creation of industry (and agriculture) the service sector cannot exist.

If those attacks are successful, they will turn like a boomerang on those who instigate them. Paradoxically those are the very people who defend the market system. In their attempts to scale back labour costs these defenders of the market system become the source of its destruction.

CHAPTER 10

RISE AND FALL OF CAPITALISM: LINEAR OR CYCLICAL?

The rise and fall of capitalism has been the subject of analysis for at least 200 years. Philosophers, economists, social scientists, and historians have developed countless theories describing how capitalism emerged and why ultimately it would be doomed. The key characteristics of these analyses are that they predict the final collapse of capitalism and its transformation into something very different in which governments (the state) will take over the command of the economy.

Karl Marx, Friedrich Engels, Joseph Schumpeter, Rosa Luxemburg, Vladimir Lenin, Karl Polanyi, all have developed what I would call 'linear theories' of the rise and fall of capitalism, i.e. theories predicting that capitalism would disappear and be replaced permanently by some form of state control over the economy. This linear theory contrasts with the cyclical theory that has been developed in this book, i.e. a theory predicting that capitalism is subject to a rise and fall followed by a resurrection, which in turn leads to a new rise and fall, ad infinitum.

In this chapter I study the different linear theories about the rise and fall of capitalism. This will allow us to shed light on the differences between the linear and cyclical views of how capitalism and the state interact.

The Predictions of Karl Marx

Karl Marx is certainly the most important and influential theorist of the rise and the demise of capitalism. Marx's analysis of the dynamics that ultimately must lead to the collapse of capitalism is based on the notion that capitalism has 'internal contradictions'. These can be described as follows. Capitalists are faced with intense competition. This competition leads them to increase the efficiency of production, which can only occur by making more investments in new machinery. As a result, production becomes more capital intensive. The same forces of competition lead capitalists to increase the degree of exploitation of workers, forcing the latter to intensify their efforts without a compensating increase in wages. This leads to an increasing degree of alienation and immiseration of workers. Thus capitalists accumulate ever more wealth and workers become poorer and poorer.

All this then sets in motion a second internal contradiction. As workers get poorer, they do not have the means to buy the products produced by capitalist firms. As a result, the profits of the capitalists tend to decline in the long run. Ultimately these contradictions must lead to the destruction of the capitalistic mode of production, when impoverished and alienated workers start a revolution against a capitalistic system that has become increasingly fragile because of its incapacity to generate sufficient profits.

After the revolution a communist mode of production will be set in motion characterized by a collectivization of the means of production. This will be the start of a 'red paradise' where the exploitation of the workers by private owners of the means of production will have become impossible.

This theory of the internal contradictions of capitalism has exerted an incredible influence on the minds of many people and has led many of them to take action so as to overthrow capitalism. This led to communist regimes in many parts of the world during the twentieth century.

It is clear, however, that the Marxian theory of the internal contra-dictions of capitalism has been rejected by the facts. There is no evidence of increasing immiseration of the workers in capitalist coun-tries. On the contrary, the workers in Europe and America where capitalism started and fully developed experienced a massive increase in real wages and economic well-being. As argued earlier, the countries in Asia that turned to capitalism in the 1970s and 1980s experienced an even higher increase of material well-being of their workers. There is in other words no evidence of ever-greater poverty of the workers in capitalistic societies; on the contrary.

The second part of the theory, that the profits of the capitalists tend to decline in the long run, has equally been rejected by the empirical evidence. There is simply no evidence that since the nineteenth cen-tury when Marx wrote his book *Das Kapital* profits of the capitalists have gone down inexorably. Capitalists' profits today are as high if not higher than in the time of Marx.

A final point to note is the following. Marx was predicting that capitalist societies would turn towards communism, and that this transformation would be permanent. The fact is that almost all coun-tries that at some point moved from capitalism into communism have now returned to capitalism. The linear Marxian theory of the demise of capitalism has been shown to be incorrect and should be rejected.

Other Linear Theories of the Demise of Capitalism

Many other theories of the demise of capitalism have been developed. They all share the same characteristic, that capitalism will disappear and be buried forever.

Marxist theorists have given us many variants of Marx's insights. Rosa Luxemburg is an outstanding representative of this school of thinking. Rosa Luxemburg was a German philosopher and economist of Polish origin who with Karl Liebknecht founded the Spartacus movement during the First World War. This led to the outbreak of the Spartacus revolution in 1918, which was violently struck down by extreme right paramilitary groups that roamed Germany after the war. Unfortunately, Rosa Luxemburg and Karl Liebknecht were murdered.

Rosa Luxemburg stressed the lack of growth in consumption in capitalist societies; itself a result of exploitation and low wages of workers. This would lead to chronic excess capacity in production, which in turn would trigger declining prices and economic depression, increasing unemployment and misery for the workers. Revolution would become inevitable. A pretty strong and simple idea.

Vladimir Lenin, the founder of the Bolshevist party in Russia, which took over power in 1917, expanded on the views of Rosa Luxemburg. In his view capitalist countries which struggled to find an outlet for their products would try to expand their markets by colonial expansion. Thus capitalism would inevitably lead to imperialism and clashes between imperialist countries in search of colonial expansion. The ensuing wars would destroy capitalism. One must admit that the World War I came close to making the Leninist prediction come true. In addition, Lenin's contribution to destroying capitalism in Russia was formidable. But again his triumph in the end would only be temporary as Russia returned to capitalism during the 1990s. This has led some to quip that communism is the longest road to capitalism.

Joseph Schumpeter, the brilliant Austrian economist, who like so many intellectuals and scientists emigrated to the US during the 1930s to escape Nazi totalitarianism, was not a communist. Yet he had an interesting theory about why capitalism was in trouble and would be overtaken by a new system of organizing the economy. Schumpeter's idea, which was developed in his book *Capitalism, Socialism and Democracy*, stressed the hostility of the intellectuals vis-à-vis a decentralized market system. As Adam Smith made clear in his celebrated 'invisible hand' analysis, the market system works in a decentralized way to bring about equilibrium between demand and supply, and does so without a central intellect guiding this quest towards the equilibrium. The self-interest of producers and consumers in competitive markets is all you need. It is a system that does not need to be centrally guided.

That is not good news for intellectuals, who like to see themselves as having superior knowledge that should be used to optimize society's well-being. These intellectuals can be dispensed with in a market system. That's why, according to Schumpeter, these intellectuals are hostile towards capitalism and will do whatever it takes to undermine the system.

This is certainly an original idea. And there can be little doubt that intellectuals in general have been hostile towards capitalism. Whether the hostility of intellectuals will lead to the demise of the system is doubtful. It certainly cannot be seen as a factor that alone will lead to the collapse of capitalism. Only if embedded in other more objective factors can it become a threat to the survival of the system.

Karl Polanyi's Prediction

Born in Vienna in 1886, Karl Polanyi was a Hungarian economist, historian, philosopher, and journalist. Yes, in those days it was possible to be all this together. With the accession of Hitler to power he lost his job in Vienna and emigrated to London and later the US and Canada. His major work was *The Great Transformation*, which combined economic, anthropological, and historical analysis of the emergence of the market system. The book also contained a prediction of the demise of that system. The prediction was based on an analysis that bears some resemblance to what we have called the internal limits of the market system.

The main ideas of Karl Polanyi can be summarized as follows. One of the essential features of the market system is that it 'commodifies' everything so as to make it tradable in markets. Labour in particular becomes a commodity like apples, pears, and sausages. As a result, the market system transfers the control of human beings' livelihoods to abstract and impersonal forces. At the same time it makes the survival of these human beings dependent on the whims of fluctuations in the markets. The protagonists of such a system see this as its main quality as it has a self-regulating dimension. Those not strong enough do not survive, but that makes the system as a whole stronger.

Clearly that is not how the people who are subjected to the movements of these markets see it. In fact this destructive self-regulating mechanism inevitably leads to a counter-movement. People hit by the blind forces of the market organize themselves using the state's power to build a protective mechanism, the most important form of which is a social security system. This protective mechanism could also take other forms such as import protection or protection against the entry of newcomers into a market.

It was the conviction of Polanyi that these protective mechanisms will destroy the market system, as they eliminate its flexibility. In particular it makes the price mechanism that should guide the system towards an equilibrium unreliable. As a result, the market system will stop producing the best possible outcome for everybody. It cannot be relied upon to produce growth and innovation. This will in the end lead to its demise as it is widely perceived to be inefficient and corrupt.

It is surprising to find that this theory has a lot of adherents today among employers who complain about protective regulations imposed by the state that make it hard if not impossible to be a dynamic entrepreneur. Polanyi would have noted that all this is inevitable in a system that treats workers as mere commodities and that overlooks the fact that they have the power to use the state to protect themselves against the blind forces of the markets.

As argued earlier, the theory developed in Chapters 3 and 4, where we discussed the internal limits of the market, is very much influenced by Polanyi's insights. These continue to be very popular.

The problem again is that Polanyi saw his prediction of the ultimate decline of capitalism in the context of a linear historical evolution. I have stressed in this book that the market system is likely to hit its limits and thus to disappear, but then only temporarily, because the state system that is likely to replace capitalism is full of 'internal contradictions' that will lead to its demise and a resurrection of the market system. This is also what the history of the last 200 years shows. This history is not linear but cyclical. Whether that will continue to be the case in the future is one of the questions we want to take up in Chapter 13.

CHAPTER 11

THE EURO IS A THREAT
TO THE MARKET SYSTEM

When the euro was introduced in 1999, few people suspected that the new monetary union the countries were entering would fundamentally change the nature of national governments in the euro countries. I will argue in this chapter that this change in the monetary regime made it much more difficult for national governments to stabilize the market system. The flipside of this was that the power of the financial markets increased to fill the gap. The euro further enhanced the trend mentioned in Chapter 1 for governments to be placed under ever more pressure from the rising market. In order to understand this it is necessary to outline a few fundamental insights into the function of a currency union.

The Eurozone Weakens National Governments

When a country becomes a member of a monetary union, it loses its own national currency and takes on the common currency. In the case of the eurozone that currency was the euro. The currency is managed by a common central bank (in the eurozone the European Central Bank, the ECB). This means that national governments, including the national central banks, lose control over the money, with several implications.[22] Here we will focus on one of those implications, possibly the most important.

The governments of countries in a monetary union have to issue their debt in a currency over which they have no control. The Belgian and Dutch governments, for example, now issue their debt in euros.

From the perspective of the national governments the euro is like a foreign currency, because they have no control over its issue. This is important because the national governments cannot offer any guarantee to bond holders that the cash (euros) will be available to pay them on the maturity date.

This contrasts with governments in countries which have their own currency. The British government (or Swedish, American, and so on) is able to give bond holders this implicit guarantee. The British government issues bonds in pounds, a currency over which the government has complete control, so in the event of a lack of pounds, it would compel the Bank of England to supply more to pay the bond holders. There is no limit to how many pounds the Bank of England can create. The British government can offer its bond holders a cast-iron guarantee. It will never end up in a situation in which it has no cash, because it is unconditionally supported by the Bank of England. This applies to stand-alone countries which issue their own currency.

The governments in the eurozone cannot offer this kind of guarantee, with the important implication that the financial markets can push national governments into insolvency against their will. This will not be immediately clear, so let us set up a scenario. We will take Spain as an example, comparing it with the United Kingdom.

Imagine that a negative economic shock affects Spain, as it did in 2010, when a deep recession was coupled with a banking crisis. The result of the shock is that the Spanish government deficit rises, also causing government debt to increase. Investors worry when they see this happen, wondering whether the Spanish government has sufficient liquidity to pay back the debt. What do investors do when they are afraid of something like this? They sell the Spanish government bonds. This sale has a dual effect. Firstly it raises the interest rate on Spanish government bonds, resulting in the Spanish government incurring higher costs when borrowing money to cover its deficit. Secondly the investors who have sold Spanish government bonds receive euros in return. They will want to reinvest those euros somewhere else and will probably go in search of bonds they have confidence in, such as German government bonds. This means that euros leave Spain and end up in Germany to be invested in German government securities, resulting in the Spanish money market drying up and the Spanish government having no money to pay out on bonds as they mature. The Spanish government finds itself in a liquidity crisis, which may force it to default.

In this scenario we encounter a self-fulfilling prophecy. Investors fear that the Spanish government will have payment problems. This leads to activity (selling) which will make their fear come true. If they had not panicked, the liquidity crisis would not have happened. This self-fulfilling process is not possible in the UK. Let us examine the same scenario. In 2010 the country was affected by a similar shock to that in Spain: a deep recession and banking crisis led to a large budget deficit and substantial rise in government debt. The development of the government debt in both countries is shown in Figure 11.1. We can see that after the deep recession of 2008–9 government debt in both

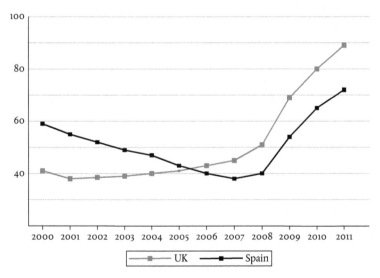

Figure 11.1. Government debt (in % GDP)

Source: European Commission, AMECO

countries began to rise steeply. We also see that government debt in the UK rose even more than that in Spain, so investors had good reason to be concerned about the British government and its capacity to pay back debt. Like the Spanish investors, they will sell their British government bonds. What effects does this have?

The first effect is parallel to what we have seen in the Spanish scenario. The interest rate on British government bonds rises. Investors who now acquire pounds for selling bonds will want to invest in government bonds they trust. In this case, however, the second effect is completely different. We assume that the choice in this scenario would also be German government bonds. In order to buy German government bonds, investors will have to sell their pounds for euros on the exchange market. This will cause the price of the pound to drop (a depreciation of the pound).

The existence of an exchange market also prevents the pounds from disappearing from the UK. The pounds which investors have sold to acquire euros now go to other investors in the same country. In contrast with Spain there is therefore no liquidity squeeze. Of course it may be that the owners of the pounds are not willing to buy British government bonds. Could the British government have liquidity problems in that case? The answer is no. The British government still has the Bank of England as backup. If it does not succeed in finding cash in the market to redeem the bonds when they mature, it will compel the Bank of England to supply those pounds, and as we stated earlier, the Bank of England can fulfil all the liquidity needs of the British government because it creates the pounds from nothing.

When we compare Spain with the UK, we see the following. Both were confronted with a similar negative shock which caused government debt to rise steeply. The difference is that the financial markets can push the Spanish government into a liquidity crisis and insolvency, whereas the same markets cannot have this effect on the British government, which has a superior weapon in the form of its own central bank to create as much money as it wants. The financial markets can push Spain or any other eurozone member state into bankruptcy, but they cannot do this to countries like the UK which issue debt in their own currency.

The difference in the way the financial markets treat the Spanish and British governments in a debt crisis is also illustrated in Figure 11.2. We can see that during the crisis the Spanish government suddenly had to pay very high interest on its bonds because investors panicked and sold Spanish bonds en masse. This did not happen in the UK, despite the fact that the British government's budget situation was no better than that of the Spanish government. Investors knew that their British government bonds were safe, so they did not sell them and the interest rate on British government securities even began to drop.

But, the reader will object, will the Bank of England's willingness to buy up British government bonds en masse and thus pump money into the economy not lead to currency depreciation (inflation)? We will return to this question in Box 11.1 at the end of the chapter.

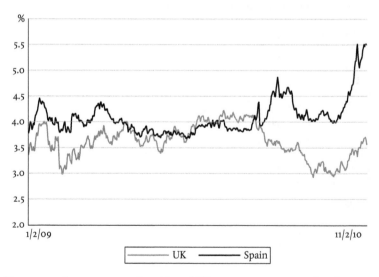

Figure 11.2. Interest rate on Spanish and UK ten-year government bonds

Source: Datastream

The panic which broke out in Spain (and other eurozone countries) in 2010 had another important consequence. The governments of the countries which encountered liquidity problems had to assemble money as quickly as they could. They were compelled to apply budgetary austerity measures as quickly as possible: taxes were raised drastically and spending was cut. This resulted in the demand for goods and services imploding and the countries concerned ended up in a new recession. The effect of austerity on output growth can be seen in Figure 11.3, with the drop in output largest in the countries where the government made the deepest spending cuts. For every percentage cut (on the horizontal axis), output dropped 1.4 per cent (vertical axis).

We are reaching the core of the problem. In a monetary union such as the eurozone the national governments are vulnerable to movements driven by fear and panic on the financial markets. This fear is fed when a country is affected by a recession. Market movements can push the governments into a liquidity crisis, which compels them to make radical spending cuts. They thus have to make cuts just when things are going badly for the economy.

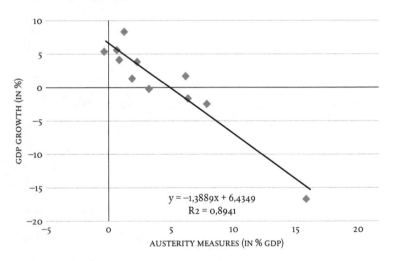

Figure 11.3. Cumulative growth in GDP and budgetary austerity 2009–12

Source: IMF, *Fiscal Observer* and European Commission, AMECO

One of the achievements of recent decades is that modern government budgets have automatic stabilizers, so that when the country enters a recession the budget automatically goes into the red because tax revenues drop and benefits payments rise. This is a stabilizing property in the budget, since during a recession the government spends more than it makes in tax revenues, ensuring that buying power in the economy is pumped up. This mitigates the recession and reduces the human suffering.

In a currency union this automatic stabilizer is switched off. The cyclical movements, the booms and busts which are so much a part of capitalism, become deeper, creating a great deal of misery. In some eurozone countries unemployment has risen to thirty per cent or higher since the euro crisis, an untenable situation, which turns many people against the market system, as was the case in the 1930s. In this sense the eurozone is a danger to the free market.

Some will say that the cold-hearted austerity programmes were necessary to restore the 'health' of government finances in those countries. In fact that has not happened, as we can see in Figure 11.4. The more extensive the austerity measures, the higher the debt ratios (the ratio of government debt to GDP). A rise in spending cuts was coupled with a rise in the debt ratio. This is related to the effect we noted previously: spending cuts lead to a sharp drop in GDP (the denominator in the debt to GDP ratio).

So the results of austerity measures (imposed by the financial markets) were not only a deep recession and a dramatic increase in unemployment, but also a steep rise in government debt ratios. The misery these countries imposed on themselves under pressure from the markets has achieved nothing. Their government debt position is worse than ever. It would take far less than this to bring the market system into discredit.

So the eurozone has a structural problem. It has seriously weakened national governments vis-à-vis the financial markets. This leads to a dangerous supremacy of the latter, which in time will undermine social consensus as to the advantages of the market system. The risk

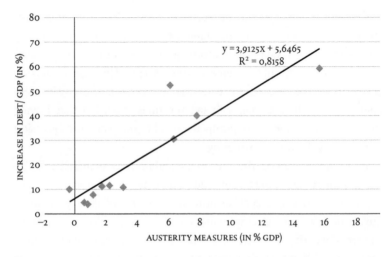

Figure 11.4. Increase in government debt/GDP (in %) and budgetary austerity (in % GDP) 2009–12

Source: IMF, Fiscal Observer, and European Commission, AMECO

is that capitalism is racing towards its limits, with all the consequences mentioned in Chapter 10.

How can we find our way out of this, saving not just the eurozone but the market itself? Here are the elements of a solution. Firstly the role of the ECB as a supporting mechanism for national governments must be tightened up. Secondly we must create a government at the level of the eurozone to take over the responsibilities of the weakened national governments.

The ECB as Lender of Last Resort

We have seen that the structural weakening of the nation states in the eurozone is caused among other things by the fact that they are no longer backed by a central bank which supports the national government in times of crisis. This means that these governments must accept the diktat of the financial markets, which would not be so bad if those markets were always right. Experience, however, shows that they are often driven by collective processes of optimism and euphoria alternating with pessimism and panic. This is not a good guide for macroeconomic policies.

It is therefore essential that the ECB take on the task fulfilled by national central banks in America and Britain. The ECB should be willing to buy up government bonds in times of crisis, when the markets panic, as they did in 2010–11. Initially the ECB was not prepared to do this. When the crisis became so intense as to threaten to destroy the eurozone, the president of the ECB, Mario Draghi, announced in 2012 that the ECB was willing to buy unlimited quantities of bonds. This purchasing programme was called Outright Monetary Transactions (OMT). This announcement had an enormous effect. Interest rates in the problem countries, which had reached record levels, dropped spectacularly (see Figure 11.5). The announcement alone was sufficient to pacify the eurozone financial markets. The ECB did not in fact need to buy any government bonds; simply announcing the policy was enough to convince many investors that it was safe to invest in Greek, Portuguese, or Spanish government bonds. This illustrates how financial markets are driven by feelings of confidence and mistrust.

There can be no doubt on this point. The ECB rescued the eurozone from collapse in 2012 by fulfilling the role of a modern central bank and supporting the national government when the financial markets were driven by fear and panic.

Sadly this is not viewed in the same light everywhere. At the beginning of 2014 the German Federal Constitutional Court decided that OMT was unconstitutional and demanded that the European Court of Justice impose strict conditions on the programme. The European court in turn ruled in 2015 that OMT does not violate the European Treaty. How the German court will react to this ruling is unclear today. A clash between the two constitutional courts is not to be excluded.

Whatever the outcome, the situation remains structurally weak. The ECB is an independent institution which cannot be controlled

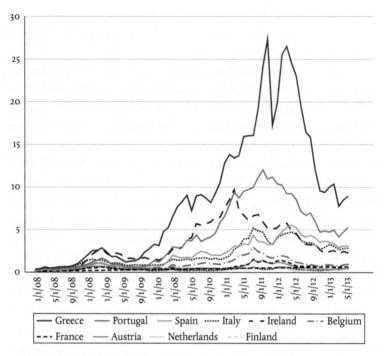

Figure 11.5. Ten-year eurozone government bond spreads

Source: Datastream. The spread is the difference between the interest rate on a country's government bonds and the interest rate on German government bonds, so it is a measure of a country's risk compared with Germany.

by national governments, in contrast with the Bank of England and the American Federal Reserve. Although these institutions are independent in outlining monetary policy, it is clear that this independence is limited. The British and American governments will not permit their own central banks to refuse support in times of financial crisis. In these countries the national governments have authority over the central banks, as they should.

In the eurozone the opposite is the case. The ECB is placed above national governments. It cannot be compelled to offer support in times of crisis. The governments are completely dependent on the good will of unelected officials. In the long run this is untenable.

The Euro is a Currency without a Country

There are only two options for solving the problem of structural weakness of national governments in the eurozone. Either we create a European government, legitimized by a European parliament, to which the national governments transfer significant budgetary authorities. This forms a political union with a European government which can directly spend money and levy taxes, and thus can issue its own debt. A government of this kind will also have the power to oblige the central bank to offer financial support. This solution makes Europe a federal state.

Willingness to realize a political union of this kind in Europe is extremely weak. Many countries are suffering from serious 'integration fatigue'. If we do not succeed in creating political union, there is only one alternative: a return to national currencies. This solution will emerge automatically because many countries will reject a system in which vital decisions are taken by anonymous and unreliable markets and unelected officials.

In Conclusion

The creation of the eurozone has led to a great shift in the power of national governments relative to the financial markets. It has seriously weakened the eurozone national governments with respect to the financial markets, leading to a dangerous supremacy of the markets, which have forced many countries in the eurozone to introduce excessive budgetary austerity measures. This in turn has led to a substantial rise in unemployment and the breakdown of parts of the social security system.

This is a dangerous tendency because in time it undermines social consensus as to the advantages of a market system. Capitalism in the eurozone threatens to reach its limits at an alarming speed, with all the consequences mentioned above.

Box 11.1. Lender of Last Resort and Inflation

When a central bank buys government bonds, it does so by issuing new money. Will this not lead to inflation and currency depreciation? This is a question asked by many people.

The answer is that in normal times excessive money creation does lead to inflation, but the times we have seen since the financial crisis of 2008 are not normal. The financial crisis was characterized by reticence on the part of the financial institutions, after the excesses of the wild bubble years, in providing credit to businesses and households. All they want is to accumulate as much liquidity as possible in order to be armed against the next crisis. They therefore sell many assets they are not 100 per cent confident about, including government bonds. This causes the prices of those assets to drop, leading to problems for many other financial institutions because the value of their assets drops too. This can result in a downward spiral, landing the economy in recession, with rising unemployment as a consequence. This is the moment at which the central bank should step in as *lender of last resort*. Buying assets, including government bonds, can stop the downward spiral.

The risk of inflation during a financial crisis is minimal, as is clear from Figure 11.6, which shows the development of the eurozone money base and money supply since 2004. Some explanation as to the concepts used here will be required. The *money base* is defined as all liquidity created by the central bank. Concretely this means banknotes and deposits which banks maintain with the central bank, the latter forming the banks' liquid reserves. The *money supply* consists of banknotes and deposits which businesses and consumers keep with the banks. This is the money with which payments are made. If there is excessive money supply, that can lead to inflation.

Let us now look in more detail at Figure 11.6. Until October 2008 the money base and money supply rose at the same pace. In October 2008 the financial crisis erupted. The ECB took its responsibility at the time and lent enormous amounts of liquidity (money base) to the banks. As we can see from Figure 11.6, the money base exploded. This was necessary in order to stop the downward spiral described above.

What happened in the meantime to the money supply (M3)? Nothing. Banks did not use the extra financial resources to grant more credit to businesses and households. They were too traumatized by the crisis and piled up the extra resources as a buffer for possible future crises. The result was that the money supply barely increased, if at all, as is clear from Figure 11.6. At no point was there a risk of increased inflation, simply because the money supply in the hands of the general public (businesses and households) did not rise.

This point is also clear from the fact that inflation in the eurozone has been dropping for several years, although the money base has increased. In 2014 inflation in the eurozone had dropped below one per cent. We now understand why. The increase in money base was necessary to prevent a deflationary spiral, but this did not lead to more credit, nor to a rise in the money supply. Most economists who work on this problem understand this. Milton Friedman, the champion of monetarism, understood this when he stated that in a financial crisis the central bank must be ready to provide liquidity for the financial system in order to prevent a deflationary spiral.[23]

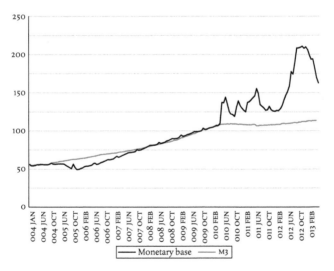

Figure 11.6. Monetary base and money supply (M3) in the eurozone (December 2009 = 100)

Source: ECB

(*Cont.*)

Box 11.1. Continued

The risk of inflation increases as the economy begins to grow faster again. At that moment the banks may use their extra cash reserves to grant too much credit. This could lead to a rapid rise in the money supply. Central banks, however, have ways of combating this effect. For instance they can sell the assets they bought during the crisis (including government bonds) back into the market, or raise the banks' minimum reserve requirements to prevent them from using their cash reserves to grant too much credit.

CHAPTER 12

THE WORLD OF PIKETTY

In 2013 the French economist Thomas Piketty wrote a remarkable book entitled *Le capital au XXIe siècle*.[24] When the English translation, *Capital in the Twenty-First Century*, was published in 2014, it became a worldwide success. For many economists this book is a milestone in economics. Piketty is already referred to as the new Marx. I have mentioned Piketty repeatedly in this book, especially when it came to the internal limits of capitalism. What is so special about his book, and what are the implications of Piketty's analysis? In this chapter we will address these questions, which will also enable us to better define the limits of capitalism.

Capital is Back

The starting point of Piketty's analysis is the long-term development of the quantity of capital in the economies of the Western world. By capital economists mean the entirety of goods and services used as factors of production, in other words used to produce new goods and services. The most important components of capital are land, natural resources, buildings, machines, and infrastructure. Capital can be private or public property. When capital is in private hands, it forms private assets. When it is in public hands it is a public asset, that is to say an asset which is the collective property of the nation.

The longest available historical records of the development of capital are for France and Great Britain, so Piketty focuses on these two countries. He also refers to other countries (the US, Germany) in his analysis, but the data generally do not go as far back.

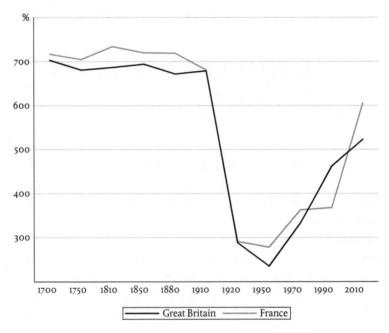

Figure 12.1. National capital in Great Britain and France (in % GDP)

Source: Piketty, http://piketty.pse.ens.fr/en/capital21c2

Figure 12.1 shows the long-term development (since 1700) of the quantity of capital in Britain and France. The quantity of capital is expressed as a percentage of national production (GDP). Note that this relates to net concepts. Piketty deducts debt from capital, so when he talks about capital it is always net capital.

We can pick out a number of remarkable phenomena in Figure 12.1. In the period from 1700 to 1910 capital was 700 per cent of GDP in both countries, and this relationship remained very stable, even during periods of great turmoil, such as the French Revolution. Throughout the entire period the capital in both countries had approximately the same value as seven years of national production.

Then something surprising happened. From 1910 the quantity of capital dropped drastically in both countries. The period of reduced capital coincided with the two world wars, which destroyed important

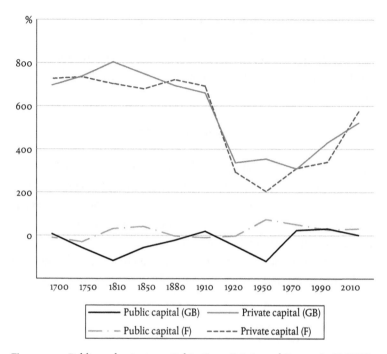

Figure 12.2. Public and private capital in Great Britain and France (in % GDP)
Source: Piketty, <http://piketty.pse.ens.fr/en/capital21c2>

parts of the capital stock. In this period, however, there was also another mechanism at work, to which we will return later. After World War II the quantity of capital began to rise dramatically. What caused these movements?

Before we answer this crucial question, let us examine Figure 12.2, which reflects the proportions of private and public capital in Britain and France during the same period. It is striking that by far the largest proportion of national capital in both countries is private capital. Public capital during most of this period is negligible. This is because Piketty works with net concepts. There is a great deal of public capital (infrastructure, for example), but there is a great deal of government debt to compensate for this. Sometimes the government's net capital is positive, sometimes negative. Since 1970 that net capital has been practically zero, in contrast with the net capital of the private sectors in Britain and France, which has been positive.

We return to the question, what are the causes of this remarkable historical development in the quantity of capital (mainly private capital)?

An Iron Law: r > g

Piketty's answer is as follows. In the very long term capital income (r) is higher than the growth of the economy (g). Expressed as a formula: r > g. This fundamental inequality, in Piketty's view, is based on historical observations spanning the last 2,000 years. Piketty has carried out substantial historical research to support this. The key findings are summed up in Figure 12.3, which reflects the historic development of r and g since the start of this time period.

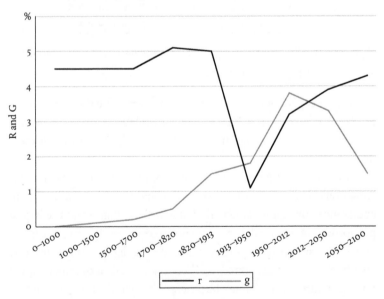

Figure 12.3. Return (after tax) on capital (r) and growth in GDP (g) in the world
Source: Piketty, <http://piketty.pse.ens.fr/en/capital21c2>

We can see that the return on capital from the start of this period until the middle of the last century was very high (between four and five per cent annually). From 1913 to the end of World War II there was a collapse of the return on capital, after which it began to rise again.

The growth of the economy follows a completely different pattern. Until the industrial revolution there was almost no growth. From the eighteenth century that growth begins to rise, reaching a peak in the period 1950–70, only to fall again. Throughout the entire period r > g, apart from in the relatively short period after World War II (1950–70). Since then we have returned to a situation in which r > g.

What is the significance of r > g? This is Piketty's answer. If the return on capital (r) is greater than the growth of GDP (g), that means that capital exhibits a tendency to rise faster than GDP. Whether that actually happens depends on the quantity saved by those who own capital. If they save little—in other words they consume most of the income they derive from their capital—then their capital will not grow quickly. If they save a lot—investing a large proportion of their income from capital—then the capital will grow quickly. The quantity of the capital with respect to GDP in the end depends on the quantity saved.*

We also see that the development from Figure 12.3 forms the basis of the developments shown in Figure 12.2. In the pre-industrial period r > g applied and capitalists saved a great deal, leading to a high ratio of capital to GDP. This inequality was disturbed in the mid-twentieth century by the two world wars, which destroyed part of the capital stock. During that period the return on capital also dropped because in many countries the taxes on income and assets rose radically (see Figure 6.2 in Chapter 6). This happened mainly due to the enormous backlash against the market system caused by the Great Depression. Clearly the system had reached its limits during the economic and

---

* It can be shown that the ratio of capital to GDP will converge to the value s/g (where s is the saving rate, i.e. savings as a proportion of GDP). So when the saving rate is fifteen per cent and economic growth is two per cent, the ratio of capital to GDP is 7.5.

financial crisis of the 1930s. As I argued above, the consequence was that governments started to play a greater role in determining the economic order, resulting in substantial increases in taxes on high incomes. In some countries, such as the United Kingdom and the United States, tax rates on top incomes rose to ninety per cent or more. This lowered the return (after taxes) on assets, because in those countries incomes from assets were taxed in the same way.

After World War II GDP growth accelerated dramatically, largely as a result of rebuilding after the horrific destruction of the war. This led to a unique combination of historically low return on capital and historically high growth. Suddenly the inequality r > g was reversed, leading to higher growth in GDP than the return on capital in this period. Wage earners whose growth in income was mainly determined by GDP growth saw their position improve, while the capitalists saw their income position deteriorate.

This did not last long, however. From the 1980s economic growth weakened, while the return on capital began to rise, mainly due to the new rise of the market system we discussed in previous chapters. Governments went out of fashion; markets were in. In many countries income taxes dropped dramatically (see Figure 6.2 in Chapter 6). In the UK and the US income taxes in the highest brackets were substantially lowered. The return on capital (after tax) rose dramatically.

It appears that the reversal in the ratio of r to g in the post-war period was a historic one-off. According to Piketty that much is clear. His argument is that we are in the process of returning to a situation which will resemble circumstances dating from the French *Ancien Régime* to the nineteenth century, when r was very high and g low. He believes that r will continue to rise, while the prospects of growth (g) are far from rosy. We are again approaching a situation in which r > g. Since owners of capital save a large proportion of their income, the capital will continue to rise in comparison with GDP.

These dynamics have a large influence on the distribution of income. In a world in which capital increases faster than GDP and return on capital is very high, an ever greater proportion of income will go to the owners of capital. If we translate this into income distribution, we can see that top earners draw in an increasingly large proportion of national income. We discussed this phenomenon in Chapter 4, where we noted (based on Piketty's historical analysis) that the top ten per cent of the income distribution have seen their share of national income rise substantially since the 1980s. This is particularly the case in the English-speaking countries. In continental European countries this increasing inequality is less pronounced (see Figure 4.2).

The *Rentiers* are Back

The dynamics which emerges from the restoration of r > g also has a further implication for society: an increasingly large proportion of the top incomes go to the *rentiers*, i.e. those who own capital. At face value that might not seem obvious, but it follows from the fact that r > g. If GDP growth is low compared with the return on (and growth of) capital, then capital becomes ever greater than GDP. This means that it becomes much easier to grow filthy rich from owning a lot of assets than from working hard. In such a world, inherited assets will also become ever greater in comparison with those which can be created by individual efforts.

In the time of Honoré de Balzac and Jane Austen ambitious young people who wanted to become rich were better off looking for rich spouses than working hard, as hard work achieved little in comparison with a good marriage. According to Piketty we are returning to a situation in which wealth is determined primarily by the family a person is born into instead of individual achievements.

To the extent that capitalism evolves towards a society in which the top one per cent (in fact the top 0.1 per cent) has become incredibly rich—not by contributing to a country's prosperity but simply by living off investments—a twofold social problem arises. Firstly, the system will be seen as unfair by most people and at a certain point they will reject it. Secondly, there is a political problem in that the super-rich exercise disproportionate influence, putting the credibility of democracy under pressure. The great inequality in assets should therefore be restricted, in order to save both democracy and capitalism. According to Piketty that can only be achieved through a tax on wealth.

A Progressive Wealth Tax

How should a wealth tax look? Ideally we would like it to hit the *rentiers*, who make no contribution to prosperity, while sparing the wealth of those who have built up their fortunes through entrepreneurship and creativity. In reality it is impossible to distinguish between the two.

This has led to the idea of introducing a progressive wealth tax. For example we might exempt wealth up to one million pounds from taxation. Many people (tradesmen, professionals, small business owners) have worked and saved hard during their lives. They have built up moderate wealth. This class of people have a great impact on the economic dynamics of a country. Taxing this fortune (given that the income from which it was accumulated has already been heavily taxed) undermines the dynamics of the market system, which in my view is best avoided.

The greater the wealth, the greater the proportion which can be seen as *rentier* wealth. So the tax rate is gradually raised. For example, between one and five million pounds a tax rate of 0.5 per cent might be applied, between five and ten million pounds one per cent, and above ten million two per cent, arriving at a rate between three and four per cent. This is just an example, and many different scales are possible. The important thing is to ensure that the phenomenally large fortunes, which almost all belong to *rentiers*, do not rise higher. If we do not do this, capitalism will collapse. A progressive wealth tax will save capitalism from the capitalists.

Criticism of Piketty

It is no surprise that there is strong criticism of Piketty. The first shot fired in the English-language world came from the *Financial Times*, which stated that Piketty had made a number of mistakes leading to an overestimation of income inequality in the United Kingdom. This led the *Financial Times* to conclude that Piketty's entire work was built on shaky ground. The storm has now died down somewhat. The current consensus is that the criticism from the *Financial Times* is exaggerated and does not undermine Piketty's conclusions. Independent estimations by Professor Tony Atkinson of Oxford University and by Professor Emmanuel Saez of the University of California, Berkeley confirm the substantial increase in income inequality in the US and the UK[25] since the start of the 1980s.

In fact there are other more serious points of criticism levelled at Piketty. I will discuss two here. A number of French economists have pointed out that the increase in capital with respect to GDP since 1950 (see Figure 12.1) is influenced by the substantial rise in real estate prices. The rise in the ratio of capital to GDP largely reflects this price effect. So rather than lots more capital having been added, the price of part of that capital (real estate) has risen substantially. That also has implications for the return on capital. The price rises on houses generate no income for those who own houses and therefore also do not cause a rise in income inequality (which nevertheless remains a fact). It is not currently clear how heavily this criticism weighs against Piketty's work. Further research will be needed to provide a definitive answer.

A second point of criticism relates to Piketty's predictions for the future development of r and g in the world. As Figure 12.3 shows, the reversal in the ratio of r to g is something which has yet to take place for the world as a whole. The figures are included in Table 12.1. Implicit in Figure 12.3 is the prediction that return on capital (after tax) will continue to rise, while the growth of the world economy will drop dramatically to 1.5 per cent per year. Piketty gives good arguments why these predictions are reasonable, but they remain questionable.

Many economists will argue that the return on capital will not continue to rise in a world of abundance of capital. There is such a thing as diminishing returns on capital. If the quantity continues to rise, sooner or later return on capital must fall too. That may be so,

Table 12.1. Return on capital (r) and growth of GDP (g) in the world

	r	g
1950–2012	3.2%	3.8%
2012–2050	3.9%	3.3%
2050–2100	4.3%	1.5%

Source: Piketty, <http://piketty.pse.ens.fr/en/capital21c2>

Piketty replies, but what is important for income distribution is the extent to which this happens. Piketty's findings are that the drop in the return on capital is not as great proportionally as the rise in the quantity of capital. In other words, if the quantity of capital rises by ten per cent, the return on capital drops by less than ten per cent. The result is that income from capital continues to rise.

Some economists, mainly the technological optimists we discussed in Chapter 5, have targeted Piketty's growth prediction. The optimists point out that growth in the world economy does not have to drop at all. This is material for further debate among economists.[†] Note, however, that the information in Table 12.1 relates to the world in its entirety. In Asia growth is still very strong. In Western Europe and America it has dropped to a maximum of two per cent per year. In this part of the world r > g is already a fact.

Ecological or Distributional Limits of Capitalism

Piketty's analysis enables us to say something about the question of which limit the market system will reach first: the ecological limit or

---

[†] The prediction that capital accumulation will continue is based on the formula $\beta = s/g$ (where β is the capital/income ratio and s is the saving rate) and the assumption that if g falls close to zero then s remains constant. That is a strong assumption. If $g = 0$ then $\beta = \infty$ but in a world of zero growth it is difficult to imagine why people would still save. So if g tends towards 0 then so does s.

Table 12.2. Share of capital belonging to the top 10% and top 1% in Europe and the US

		France	UK	US	Europe
Top 10%	1810	79.9%	82.9%	58.0%	82.2%
	2010	62.4%	70.5%	71.5%	63.9%
Top 1%	1810	45.6%	54.9%	25.0%	52.1%
	2010	24.4%	28.0%	33.8%	24.4%

Source: Piketty, <http://piketty.pse.ens.fr/en/capital21c2>

the distributional limit. According to Piketty growth will drop further. That is good for the environment but bad for distribution. After all, low growth raises the ratio of capital to GDP, further encouraging a society in which the *rentiers* accumulate large fortunes. In this case we will come to the distributional limit first.

I consider this interpretation problematic. In the West we live in a democracy. It is highly unlikely that we will return to the *Ancien Régime* in which inequality of wealth and income was even greater than it is today. This is apparent from Table 12.2. At the start of the nineteenth century the top ten per cent owned approximately eighty per cent (the top one per cent around fifty per cent) of all the wealth in Europe. Rather counterintuitively, America was much more egalitarian than Europe at the time, as observed by Alexis de Tocqueville on his visit to the country.[‡] The top ten per cent owned 'only' fifty-eight per cent of the total wealth, with the top one per cent owning twenty-five per cent.

In Europe inequality of wealth distribution is now significantly lower than at the start of the nineteenth century. In the US, on the other hand, wealth inequality has risen, although it is still lower than in Europe in the early nineteenth century.

[‡] Alexis de Tocqueville, *De la démocratie en Amérique*. According to de Tocqueville a democracy can only function if society is sufficiently equal.

The *Ancien Régime* was an authoritarian regime which maintained great wealth inequality by force. Today's democratic states are not likely to let matters go so far, because at a certain point a majority will elect politicians who redistribute wealth. As I argued above, this development will depend to a large extent on the way in which democratic societies work. If they are of the inclusive type, my conclusion is probable. However, if they adhere to the exclusive type, the conclusion could be called into question.

CHAPTER 13

PENDULUM SWINGS
BETWEEN MARKETS AND
GOVERNMENTS

The history of the past 200 years is one of large pendulum swings in the scope of markets and governments. The question now is whether these swings will continue to repeat themselves in the future. If that is the case, the expansion of the markets we have seen in the last thirty years will inevitably lead to governments making a comeback as the guiding force in the economy.

The Financial Crisis: Turning Point in the
Rise of the Market?

The financial and economic crisis of 1929 was an important milestone in the rise of government in large parts of the world, leading to a dramatic and long-lasting drop in national production in many countries and to mass unemployment in the industrial world. These dramatic developments brought the free market system into discredit. Driven by protest among the people and social instability the national governments in many countries took over the reins of the economy. The question now is whether the banking crisis of 2008 can lead to the same turnaround.

The financial crisis of 2008 had the same cause as the crash of 1929. In both cases there was a period of great euphoria beforehand, which drove companies and households to invest and consume. Banks went along with this and encouraged investments and consumption through cheap credit. Large debts piled up, until the house of cards collapsed.

The aftermath periods to the 1930s crash and the recent crisis, however, have been completely different, as shown in Figure 13.1. This shows the monthly development of worldwide industrial production from the beginning of the two crises (June 1929 and April 2008). The difference is remarkable. Whereas in the 1930s industrial production continued to drop until around forty months after the start of the 1929 crisis, around twelve months after April 2008 industrial production began to rise again. The initial drop in production was just as substantial immediately after both historical episodes, but the recovery after the 2008 crisis started much earlier than it did after the crisis of 1929. Why is that?

The answer is that economists and policy makers have learnt from the mistakes of the 1930s depression, when the governments responded in completely the wrong way. Instead of pumping money into the economy when the financial crisis erupted in 1929, national banks in many countries tightened up on credit, resulting in more banks folding and large sections of the economy collapsing into bankruptcy.*

The governments made similar mistakes. When government revenues dropped as a result of reduced production and the budget deficit increased, governments attempted to maintain balance in the budget by raising taxes and reducing spending. That exacerbated the economic collapse.

After the banking crisis of 2008 the central banks and governments in most countries responded completely differently. The central banks all pumped lots of money into the economy while governments permitted rises in the budget deficit. This soon put a stop to the

---

* It is worth noting that Milton Friedman, the father of monetarism, popularized this criticism in his book (co-written with Anna Jacobson Schwartz) *A Monetary History of the United States, 1867–1960* (Princeton, NJ: Princeton University Press, 1963). According to Friedman the US Federal Reserve made the mistake of pumping too little money into the economy, making the Great Depression in the US much worse.

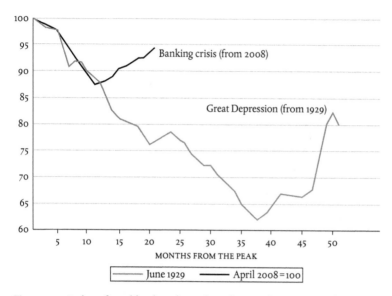

Figure 13.1. Index of worldwide industrial production during two recessions

Source: Barry Eichengreen and Kevin O'Rourke, 'A Tale of Two Depressions', *VoxEU* (8 March 2010), <http://www.voxeu.org/article/tale-two-depressions-what-do-new-data-tell-us-february-2010-update>

downward spiral, avoiding a second Great Depression. Perhaps surprisingly, it can therefore be argued that the authorities (central banks and governments) rescued the free market system by their responses after 2008.

Compared with the other industrialized countries, the eurozone recovered less effectively after the financial crisis of 2008, as can be seen in Figure 13.2, which compares the development of GDP in the eurozone with that of the UK and the US. It is remarkable that the Great Recession of 2008–9 had approximately the same intensity in these three economies, whereas the progression was different after 2009. While the UK and US saw a recovery (albeit a slow one), the eurozone slid back into recession in 2011–12. This recession was particularly deep in the southern eurozone countries (plus Ireland) and led to a dramatic rise in unemployment. In some countries, such

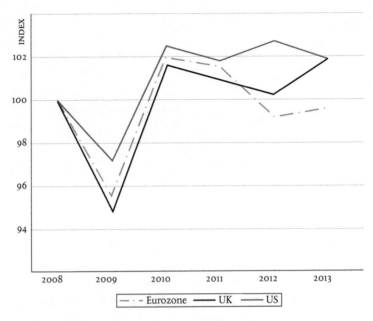

Figure 13.2. GDP in constant prices (year 2008 = 100)

Source: European Commission, AMECO database

as Greece and Spain, unemployment rose above thirty per cent, a situation reminiscent of the Great Depression of the 1930s.

This second recession in the eurozone is the result of the structural problem in the currency union identified in Chapter 12. The absence of central banks to support national governments led to panic in many markets and forced the governments to implement overly strict austerity measures.[26] This in turn led to a sharp drop in the total demand for goods and services at a point when the economy had yet to recover. The consequence was a double-dip recession, in which governments failed to maintain control over their budget deficits, and government debt ratios also rose sharply, because GDP (the denominator in this ratio) shrank. So the perverse thing about this policy was not only that unemployment increased dramatically, but also that the burden of government debt rose, to such an extent that some eurozone countries now carry an unbearable government debt which condemns them to walk the path of austerity for decades to come. It is unclear whether the populations of these countries will be prepared to do that. The eurozone policy makers failed to learn the lesson of the 1930s.

Finally we can state that for most countries in the world it is unlikely that the crisis of 2008 was a turning point akin to that of 1929. In certain eurozone countries (especially the countries on the periphery) that is less clear and a rejection of the free market cannot be ruled out, but apart from these countries an event of that nature looks unlikely today.

Are the Pendulum Swings inevitable?

Prediction is difficult, especially if it's about the future, Niels Bohr, the great Danish physicist once said, so I will avoid embarking on predictions myself. What I can do is sketch two scenarios, one pessimistic and one optimistic. I leave it to the reader to make a choice.

Yes, there will always be Pendulum Swings

There are two reasons for pessimism. The growing importance of the market since the 1980s will inevitably be abruptly cut back. We explored the mechanisms for this in previous chapters. Their destructive work continues as I write.

The environment represents an external limit, towards which the free market system is heading at full speed. Over the last few decades material production has risen exponentially. There has been almost no change to this in the last ten years, other than in the developed countries, where growth has slowed. The developing countries, however, have taken over in carrying the torch of economic growth (see Figure 13.3). That is both good and bad news at the same time. Good news because it draws millions of people out of poverty, but bad news because the pressure on the environment is not reduced. In fact the

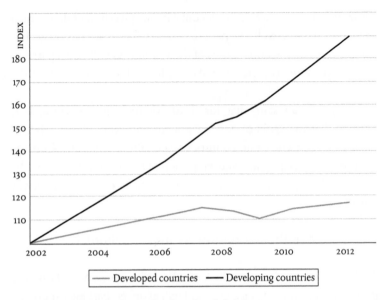

Figure 13.3. Index of GDP in developed and developing countries
Source: World Bank

billions of people whose consumption level today is barely ten per cent that of the rich West will not stop production until they approach Western consumption levels.

The damage to the environment is increasing mainly because governments are failing to pass on the external costs of this material production to those who generate them. I explained in Chapter 6 why governments fail. Governments, which in principle should defend the collective good, lose out to private interested parties, who do everything in their power to resist restrictions on their activities.

The problem is most prominent when it comes to CO_2 emissions, which continue unabated. The world is heading straight for an environmental catastrophe of unprecedented proportions. The inevitability of such a catastrophe relates to nonlinearities of the ecosystem, as discussed in Chapter 3. In the pessimistic scenario we are outlining here, let us assume that those nonlinearities really exist. So if CO_2

emissions continue to rise, at a certain point we will reach a tipping point (see Figure 3.1). From then on global warming will accelerate rapidly, resulting in large parts of the world becoming uninhabitable. Since change beyond such a tipping point is very rapid, we will have no time to adapt. Agricultural land, water, and food will become scarce. This will inevitably lead to serious conflicts between countries fighting for survival. The market system will be obliterated.

The other limit of the market system, as we mentioned earlier, is an internal one. It relates to inequality of income and wealth. The market system is indifferent to the degree of inequality. In Chapter 4 we showed that even if the market has achieved equilibrium, it can conceal great inequality, leaving many people with insufficient living resources or none at all. Such dramatic situations leave the market unmoved.

For many people, however, an equilibrium of this kind is unacceptable. This applies firstly to those excluded by the market system and secondly to those who do well but who reject the situation because they consider it unfair. The latter group also wants to fight for a different balance, in which there is space for those who are excluded from the market system. If the inequality is great enough, this can lead to a rejection of the market system.

Figure 13.4 reveals a similar dynamic to that in Figure 3.1. The horizontal axis shows inequality and the vertical axis shows social and political instability. When inequality increases, so does the degree of political and social instability. At B we have reached a tipping point. Great inequality leads to revolution, violently overturning the market system. From that point on the degree of inequality is dramatically reduced. Such revolutions, however, do not always lead to reduced instability; in fact instability may initially rise, because many conflicting groups attempt to grasp power. In time this tends to lead to consolidation of power in the hands of an authoritarian regime. The cycle can begin again.

The question we must explore here is whether capitalism in 2016 exhibits a trend of ever rising inequality. In Chapters 4 and 12 we saw

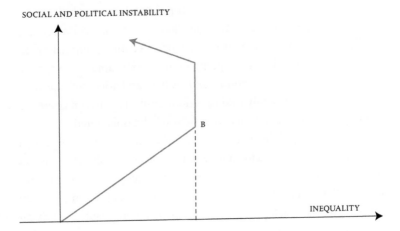

Figure 13.4. Inequality and instability

that in many countries, especially the Anglo-Saxon countries, there are clear signs of continually rising inequality. We have also established that this dynamics is at work in continental Europe, albeit in a less dramatic manner.

We might also formulate the question as follows: is the tendency towards greater inequality a temporary phenomenon? In that case we need not worry too much. The process will stop in time, before we reach point B in Figure 13.4, in which case the market system will not come up against its internal limit.

Was Karl Marx Right After All?

Alternatively, however, the tendency towards increasing inequality since the 1980s might continue, because, as we now know, there is a rule of capitalism which makes the system ever more unequal. That was also the vision of Karl Marx, who thought that this trend would inevitably lead to revolution and the overturn of capitalism. Are we really moving in that direction, and will Karl Marx turn out to have been right?

Before we answer the question, it should be noted that Marx was both right and wrong. In the nineteenth century he predicted that capitalism would be overturned, mainly because the system condemned millions of people to ever increasing poverty. This overturn took place in a number of important countries (Russia, China), but not in many others, which in fact were further advanced in their capitalist development. Marx painted a picture in which capitalism would collapse, after which communism would reign for eternity. A return to capitalism was not possible according to this linear trend line. Well, for almost all the countries which have tried communism that has not turned out to be the case. As we argued earlier, history takes more of a cyclical than a linear course, because the political system that wins against the market system eventually also comes up against its own limits. The fate of Russian and Chinese communism, where the government took over all economic power, is a spectacular example of this.

But let us return to the question: does the current tendency towards increasing inequality entail a law which will lead to point B in Figure 13.4? It is a very tricky question, which leads to widely varying answers.

In Chapter 12 we outlined the ideas of Thomas Piketty. In his view the answer to this question is decidedly yes. The tendency towards increasing inequality since the 1980s will continue. According to Piketty there is no mechanism in capitalism to stop this trend.

Piketty formulates an important insight into the long-term tendency of capitalism. If that is correct and income inequality is to increase further, then it is almost inevitable that capitalism will clash with its internal limits. Many people will begin to resist the tendency for a small elite to acquire such a large proportion of the income and wealth, as was the case with the *Ancien Régime*. This will lead us to point B in Figure 13.4, as happened in the first half of the twentieth century when large parts of the world (Russia and its neighbours, China under Mao's leadership, India with its five-year plans) turned their backs on capitalism. It will happen again if the tendency towards inequality persists. In this scenario we are therefore moving inevitably towards the overturn of the market system and a new triumph for governments, until they too reach their limits. And so the cycle continues.

In this doomsday scenario it therefore does not look good for the future of the market system, which will inevitably come up against its limits and be scaled back.

A Reformist Scenario

There is, however, the possibility of an alternative, less invasive scenario. In this reformist scenario forces arise in society which put a brake on the rush of capitalism towards its limits.

Let us first talk about income inequality. In this scenario great pressure is placed on governments to raise taxes on the top incomes and wealth. The fundamental pressure to achieve a more fair distribution forces governments to raise taxes on very high incomes and wealth, making inequality less extreme and more acceptable to society once again. This is in fact the scenario which occurred from the 1930s in those parts of the world which did not convert to communism. Tax rates of ninety per cent and above on top incomes were the rule at the time in countries such as the UK and the US. In many European countries, too, incomes above a certain level were largely siphoned off. Many countries introduced taxes on wealth. This strategy caused the free market system to come up against its limits, but softly. Governments may have been more important, but the foundation of the market system was not destroyed, as it was in the countries which adopted communism.

From the 1980s taxes on top incomes dropped dramatically, but there is no reason why we should not raise them substantially again today. The criticism of this approach is that such high taxes would have negative economic effects. People who earn millions would make less effort and show less initiative, but we have seen in previous chapters that there are few indications that this is the case.

A similar reformist scenario could also slow the movement of capitalism towards its *external* limits. In this scenario people will put pressure on governments to combat pollution, for instance with taxes, and regulations on harmful emissions (CO_2 in the first instance), taxing fossil fuels, and subsidizing alternative energy sources. This can call a halt to the degradation of the environment.

Two conditions must be fulfilled in order to achieve this optimistic scenario. Firstly the democratic institutions within countries must function well enough. That is necessary both for reducing inequality and for improving the environment. Those democratic institutions must ensure that the interests of the lower-income classes are served just as well as those of the top earners. As stated, that is not currently the case in many rich countries.

The interests of the many who suffer from environmental damage must also be taken care of. Democratic institutions ensure that these people are represented just as well as those who have caused harm. Democracy is therefore more effective than authoritarian regimes at protecting the market system from itself.

A second condition for giving this reformist scenario a chance is that countries should be prepared to work together. This applies both to environmental problems and to inequality.

In order to implement taxation policies with the aim of capping top incomes, international collaboration is required. If France is the only country to tread this path, countries such as the United Kingdom will stand ready to roll out the red carpet for rich French individuals, as British prime minister David Cameron announced after the vote on taxing high incomes in the French National Assembly. Raising taxes on high incomes in one country leads to gains for those countries which do not implement such a policy. This can only be avoided through international collaboration, which does not seem likely to materialize in the immediate future.

A similar problem arises for environmental policy, which is particularly pronounced in the case of CO_2 emissions. Without international collaboration a free-rider problem arises. If Europe taxes emissions, other countries benefit from reduced emissions while having less action to take themselves. In time Europe, which bears high costs (in the form of loss of industrial competitiveness due to a tax on CO_2), will be forced to forgo its CO_2 tax. So nothing happens, or far too little.

We can therefore conclude that if these two conditions are not met, the market system is heading towards its two limits: those of external costs and those of internal unsustainable income inequality.

A Sombre Future?

It does not currently look like these two conditions will be met. That might sound pessimistic, but I fear that it is the reality. The question which then arises is which of the two limits will be reached first?

It is very difficult to answer this question with our current knowledge. After all, it is a matter of timing. We can say with great certainty that capitalism will reach its limits if we do not succeed in implementing the reformist programme. When that might happen, however, is much more difficult to predict. We still know too little about the environmental effects of CO_2 emissions or the timing of possible tipping points. Will they emerge within a decade or half a century?

When it comes to the effects of great income inequality on the fabric of society and government and the danger of revolutionary dynamics, we are again groping in the dark. We know from history that excessive inequality eventually leads to great upheaval, but we know less about the precise timing of this trend.

However, it seems probable that the external limits of the market system (imposed by the environment) will be reached sooner than the internal limits (caused by great inequality), as explained in Chapter 12. Democratic states have relatively strong internal stabilizers to ensure that large income and wealth inequalities are corrected in time. These seem to be lacking for environmental problems, which tend to cross borders.

The Myth of Sisyphus

Sisyphus was a Greek king who felt stronger and wiser than Zeus, and was punished for his hubris. He was sentenced to push a rock up a mountain every day, after which the rock would roll back down each evening. The following day Sisyphus had to start all over again, continuing for eternity.

In his essay *The Myth of Sisyphus* Albert Camus gave an existentialist interpretation of this well-known Greek myth. Camus sees Sisyphus's punishment as a metaphor for the absurdity of life. How should we deal with this absurdity, he wonders? One option is to commit suicide. Camus rejects this option. Instead he suggests that we should rebel against the absurdity of life by throwing ourselves into it, living intensely, and being creative. The revolutionary hero is the one who despite the absurdity and knowing that his rebellion will eventually achieve nothing, still sets the rock in motion and remains happy. 'Il faut s'imaginer Sisyphe heureux' ('One must imagine Sisyphus happy'), Camus decided.

That is the position I would like to offer as a guiding principle for the end of this book. It will be extraordinarily difficult to prevent future catastrophes. It may even already be too late. (I am at least a little more optimistic than Albert Camus with his Sisyphus interpretation, which is very bleak indeed.) We have a small chance of preventing decline with the reforms I outlined above. But even if that does not work, we are left with the option of doing as Sisyphus did, of starting again each day. It is the only way of giving meaning to our existence.

If we do not take action, our grandchildren will not forgive us for failing to try to save them. That in itself is sufficient motivation to persist.

NOTES

1. See Kahneman's bestseller *Thinking Fast and Slow* (London: Allen Lane, 2011). See also <http://www.amacad.org/binaries/video/streamPlayer.aspx?i=188>.
2. Antonio Damasio, *Descartes' Error: Emotion, Reason, and the Human Brain* (New York: Putnam, 1994).
3. See Björn Lomborg, *Cool It: The Skeptical Environmentalist's Guide to Global Warming* (New York: Alfred Knopf, 2007).
4. For a thorough analysis of scenarios see the report by the Intergovernmental Panel on Climate Change, 2014, <http://www.ipcc.ch/report/ar5/wg2>.
5. See for example <http://www.iflscience.com/environment/climatologist-arctic-carbon-release-could-mean-"were-fucked">.
6. Jared Diamond, *Collapse: How Societies Choose to Fail or Succeed* (New York: Viking, 2005).
7. See Alan Greenspan, *The Age of Turbulence: Adventures in a New World* (London: Allen Lane, 2007).
8. Carmen M. Reinhardt and Kenneth S. Rogoff, *This Time is Different: Eight Centuries of Financial Folly* (Princeton, NJ: Princeton University Press, 2009).
9. Michael J. Sandel, *What Money Can't Buy: The Moral Limits of Markets* (London: Allen Lane, 2012).
10. Kenneth J. Arrow, 'Gifts and exchanges', *Philosophy and Public Affairs*, 1/4 (1972), pp. 343–62.
11. Ronald Coase, 'The Nature of the Firm', *Economica*, 4/16 (November 1937), pp. 386–405.
12. See Frans de Waal, *Our Inner Ape: The Best and Worst of Human Nature* (London: Granta Books, 2005). See also Matt Ridley, *The Origins of Virtue* (London: Penguin Books, 1996).
13. Erik Brynjolfsson and Andrew McAfee, *Race Against the Machine: How the Digital Revolution is Accelerating Innovation, Driving Productivity, and Irreversibly Transforming Employment and the Economy* (Lexington, MA: Digital Frontier Press, 2012).
14. Robert Skidelsky and Edward Skidelsky, *How Much is Enough? The Love of Money, and the Case for the Good Life* (London: Allen Lane, 2012).
15. Facundo Alvaredo, Tony Atkinson, Thomas Piketty, Emmanuel Saez, and Gabriel Zucman, *The World Wealth and Income Database* (WID), <http://www.wid.world>, and Tony Atkinson and Salvatore Morelli, *The Chartbook of Income*

Inequality, VoxEU (2014), <http://www.voxeu.org/article/chartbook-economic-inequality>.

16. See Raghuram G. Rajan and Luigi Zingales, *Saving Capitalism from the Capitalists* (New York: Crown Business, 2003), and Thomas Piketty, *Capital in the Twenty-First Century*, trans. Arthur Goldhammer (Cambridge, MA: Belknap Press, 2014).

17. Jonathan D. Ostry, Andrew Berg, and Charalambos G. Tsangarides, *Redistribution, Inequality, and Growth*, IMF Staff Discussion Note (April 2014), <https://www.imf.org/external/pubs/ft/sdn/2014/sdn1402.pdf>.

18. Mancur Olson, *The Logic of Collective Action: Public Goods and the Theory of Groups* (Cambridge, MA: Harvard University Press, 1965).

19. Daron Acemoglu and James A. Robinson, *Why Nations Fail: The Origins of Power, Prosperity and Poverty* (London: Profile, 2012).

20. Martin Gilens, *Affluence and Influence: Economic Inequality and Political Power in America* (Princeton, NJ: Princeton University Press; New York: Russell Sage Foundation, 2012).

21. André Sapir, 'Globalisation and the reform of European social models', *Journal of Common Market Studies*, 44/2 (June 2006), pp. 369–90, <http://bruegel.org/2005/09/globalisation-and-the-reform-of-european-social-models> and Tito Boeri, *Let Social Policy Models Compete and Europe Will Win*, paper presented at a conference hosted by the John F. Kennedy School of Government, Harvard University, 11–12 April 2002.

22. For a thorough analysis see Paul De Grauwe, *Economics of Monetary Union* (11th edn, Oxford: Oxford University Press, 2016).

23. Milton Friedman and Anna Jacobson Schwartz, *A Monetary History of the United States, 1867–1960* (Princeton, NJ: Princeton University Press, 1963).

24. Thomas Piketty, *Le capital au XXIe siècle* (Paris: Editions du Seuil, 2013); Eng. *Capital in the Twenty-First Century*, trans. Arthur Goldhammer (Cambridge, MA: Harvard University Press, 2014).

25. Odran Bonnet, Pierre-Henri Bono, Guillaume Camille Chapelle, and Étienne Wasmer, 'Capital is not back: A comment on Thomas Piketty's "Capital in the 21st Century"', *VoxEU* (30 June 2014), <http://www.voxeu.org/article/housing-capital-and-piketty-s-analysis>.

26. Paul De Grauwe and Yuemei Ji, 'Panic-driven austerity in the Eurozone and its implications', *VoxEU* (21 February 2013), <http://www.voxeu.org/article/panic-driven-austerity-eurozone-and-its-implications>.

INDEX

Note: text within tables, figures, and boxes is indicated by *t*, *f*, and *b* following the page number. Footnotes are indicated by 'n'.

Acemoglu, D. 77
Africa 42*b*, 78
Ancien Régime 141–2, 151
Anglo-Saxon countries 42–3*b*, 63, 93, 150
Aristotle 61
Arrow, K. 46
art 46 61
  bubbles 47
Asia 7, 42–3*b*
Atkinson, T. 63–4, 139
Austria
  eurozone government bond spreads, ten-year 126*f*
  labour costs, gross hourly 101*f*
  social security spending as percentage of government spending 84*f*
authoritarian regimes 80, 142, 149
automatic stabilizers 123

banking system and external risk effects 30
bankruptcy/insolvency 31, 120, 144
Belgium
  employer contribution and labour costs 107
  eurozone government bond spreads, ten-year 126*f*
  labour costs, gross hourly 101*f*
Bohr, N. 147
booms and busts 28–9, 31–2, 37, 123
Brynjolfsson, E. 57
budgetary austerity measures 119, 123, 124*f*, 127, 146–7
Bulgaria 82
  labour costs, gross hourly 101*f*
busts *see* booms and busts

Camus, A. 155
capital
  accumulation 140n
  diminishing returns 139
  /income ratio 140n
  public and private in Great Britain and France 133*f*
  quantity of 131–5, 140
capitalism 3, 7, 8, 18, 28–9
  crony 77, 78
  global 43*b*
  internal contradictions 112–13, 116
  linear theories *see* linear theories on the rise and fall of capitalism
  see also capitalism, limits of
capitalism, limits of 11–18
  individual and collective rationality 13–14
  see also external limits of capitalism; internal limits of capitalism
carbon dioxide emissions 22–4, 26, 148–9
  and emission standards 66–8
  and taxation 153–4
central banks 144–5
  see also in particular Bank of England *under* United Kingdom; European Central Bank (ECB); Federal Reserve (Fed) *under* United States
centrally planned economic model 6–7
China
  consumption per capita 62
  gross domestic product (GDP) per capita 2*f*
climate change 26
  see also global warming
Club of Rome, 'The Limits to Growth' 25n
Coase, R. 49
collective decision-making process 34–5
collective irrationality 20